D1274945

Kaizen Strategies
for Successful
Organizational Change

In an increasingly competitive world, it is quality of thinking that gives an edge. An idea that opens new doors, a technique that solves a problem, or an insight that simply helps make sense of it all.

We work with leading authors in the fields of management and finance to bring cutting-edge thinking and best learning practice to a global market.

Under a range of leading imprints, including *Financial Times Prentice Hall,* we create world-class print publications and electronic products giving readers knowledge and understanding which can then be applied, whether studying or at work.

To find out more about our business and professional products, you can visit us at *www.business-minds.com*

For other Pearson Education publications, visit *www.pearsoned-ema.com*

Kaizen Strategies
for Successful
Organizational Change

ENABLING EVOLUTION AND
REVOLUTION WITHIN
THE ORGANIZATION

———

Michael Colenso

Pearson Education Limited

Head Office:
Edinburgh Gate
Harlow CM20 2JE
Tel: +44 (0)1279 623623
Fax: +44 (0)1279 431059

London Office:
128 Long Acre, London WC2E 9AN
Tel: +44 (0)171 447 2000
Fax: +44 (0)171 240 5771
Website: www.business-minds.com

First published in Great Britain 2000

© Pearson Education Limited 2000

The right of Michael Colenso to be identified as author of this work has been
asserted by him in accordance with the Copyright, Designs, and Patents Act 1988.

ISBN: 0 273 63985 4

British Library Cataloguing in Publication Data
A CIP catalogue record for this book can be obtained from the British Library.

10 9 8 7 6 5 4 3 2 1

Typeset by M Rules
Printed and bound in Great Britain by Biddles Ltd, Guildford & King's Lynn

The Publishers' policy is to use paper manufactured from sustainable forests.

CONTENTS

CHAPTER 13

Why Change Goes Wrong and What to Do About It   169

PREFACE

This book and its sibling *Kaizen Strategies for Improving Team Performance*, were commissioned by Financial Times Prentice Hall to augment three earlier titles on *Kaizen*[1] which were published in 1995. All five books have been written by associates or employees of the Europe Japan Centre. All five books differ somewhat from other *Kaizen* titles in that they try to relate *Kaizen* to the Western business environment rather than presenting *Kaizen* in detail as a business philosophy. It is perhaps for this reason that the original titles in the series have done rather well.

Awareness of *Kaizen* is extremely high in the West and many of its precepts and processes are widely used. In general it is believed to be a Japanese system for continuous quality improvement as indeed it is. *Kaizen* holds much more for the management of an organization though. It takes the need for continuous quality improvement as a given, as a ticket to the game, as a licence to play rather than as a basis for competitive differentiation. All the organizations with which the Europe Japan Centre works by and large agree with this precept; in the modern competitive climate how can an organization think otherwise?

What distinguishes *Kaizen* is that it enables the delivery of TQM on the one hand, but it also offers a rich kit of supervisory and managerial competencies which shape a different organizational culture and supports it with highly effective operating tools. Using and applying those tools in the pursuit of continuous improvement invests an organization with powerful process skills which, as people like Honda have shown, provide a measure of organizational strength which extends beyond the making of quality products into the area of strategic differentiation.

This book deals with change. Installing a *Kaizen* operating philosophy in an organization is about the most radical and far-reaching change any management will confront. So I have included a chapter on how to do it, and I hope you will not find it daunting.

For the rest I have tried to do three things.

- First I have tried to show how organizational strategy is changing in response to a turbulent and competitive operating climate. I have found this a necessary starting point because I hold the view that there is only one reason to make changes in an organization and that is to support and enable its strategy. You will find this view repeated with almost mantra-like frequency in this book.

- Second I have also tried to deal with the main tools and levers of change and offered advice on how best to deploy them.

- Third I have shown, where appropriate, what *Kaizen* offers in each of these change arenas.

In writing this book I have been consistently reminded about how difficult it is to manage change painlessly. But I am also compelled by how necessary it is to build robust organizations able to deal competently and assuredly with change. What has emerged is a concern that in the West we still regard change as a series of initiatives, and indeed I have used that word very often in the book and provided a lot of case examples of successful initiatives.

The organization of the future must be designed to adapt consistently and fast to a changing environment. One is looking for accelerated Darwinism, but accelerated to break-neck speed. Inevitably this has involved me in the revolution/evolution debate. I think this is pretty tedious stuff for it is predicated on the premise that one precludes the other. I hope Chapter 12, *The Responsive Organization,* helps people break out of the sterility and limitation of this argument and look to build a new kind of organization. *Kaizen* provides an excellent base for this sort of organization.

I have been well supported by my colleagues at the Europe Japan Centre in writing this book. Particularly I owe thanks to Chris Patrick whose laconic but trenchant e-mails are masterpieces of the genre. I want also to thank Pat Wellington who has been of great personal support to me and provided me with a wider range of testing opportunities than I might otherwise have sought.

Authorship is a lonely activity and those closest to you bear the brunt of re-integrating you into the social world after a day spent in communion with a cathode ray tube. My thanks to Joan, my wife, who has mastered the art of gentle re-entry into the real world; without this one might simply become an electronic anchorite.

Authors also love to know what people feel and think about their books so please drop me a line on 101733.2337@compuserve.com

Michael Colenso

1.　Barnes: *Kaizen Strategies for Successful Leadership;* Cane: *Kaizen Strategies for Winning Through People;* Wellington: *Kaizen Strategies for Customer Care.*

ABOUT THE EUROPE JAPAN CENTRE

THE EUROPE JAPAN CENTRE IS part of the Osaka Gas Group, a major Japanese company that has global interests and information collection abilities that enable the Centre to keep up to date with the best management practices worldwide. We offer a range of services to organizations anywhere in the world, based around the twin pillars of human resources/management development and market research.

We have been in existence since 1991, and have gained an excellent reputation in a broad cross-section of sectors, including public and private organizations, large companies and SMEs, and industrial, commercial and service organizations.

Human Resources Development

Within the human resources area, the Europe Japan Centre focuses on the management of change, based on team development and the concept of *Kaizen* (continuous improvement). We are fortunate to have had in our team one of the last remaining members of Dr Deming's team, who worked with Deming for ten years in Japan and was therefore at the forefront of the whole quality movement.

'*The best of East and West*' is our philosophy, and our research department constantly gathers best practice information for us to use in our consultancy work. We are geared to achieving practical results. Our educational programmes are based on ideas and techniques which have been shown to work. By letting managers see how they can close the gap between concepts and action, we can help to change attitudes and to create an environment where people become more self-motivated, thus helping to bring about a more effective and innovative organization.

Our human resources consultancy offers the following services.

- **Top quality seminars and workshops**: these are led by experts in their own fields of knowledge, or by experienced HR consultants who can convey their ideas in a clear and stimulating manner.

Topics evolve continuously, reflecting our position as a leading consultancy aware of the latest trends in management thinking and practice, not only in the UK but worldwide.

- **In-house training programmes**: we have worked with a wide variety of companies to help them introduce new ways of working, including the introduction of *Kaizen* (continuous improvement) techniques, team-working, strategies for innovation, etc., programmes can be short and concentrated or spread over a number of months or even years. Typical projects include initial work with senior management, followed by workshops, practical sessions and training the trainers.

- **World class speakers**: we can provide a range of speakers with the 'added extra' whether from business, or the worlds of sport, entertainment or the media – to give an event excitement and make it live longer in the minds of audiences.

- **Event management and administration**: we are happy to work as the marketing arm of organizations arranging seminars, conferences or other events. Our staff understand the importance of treating each organization's clients as we would do our own, i.e. as very special people.

Research

The second main area of the Europe Japan Centre's business is research. We focus mainly on market research either to assist European companies to enter and operate successfully in Japan and China, or to help Japanese companies within European markets. Our network of researchers in Europe and Asia means we have access to the latest on-the-spot information, and that we can conduct surveys or give advice rapidly and accurately.

For more information or to arrange an informal meeting, please contact Pat Wellington or Catherine Davis at:

The Europe Japan Centre, Mutual House, 70 Conduit Street, London W1R 9TQ; tel: + 44 (0)207 287 8605; fax: + 44 (0)207 287 8607; email: *info@ejc.co.uk*

Or consult our website: *http://www.ejc.co.uk*

CHAPTER 1

About Change

Introduction

———

Why Does Change Fail?

———

Belief as the Precursor to Change

———

Change and the Contemporary Operating Climate

———

Designing the Modern Organization

———

Kaizen's Particular Contribution

———

The Purpose of All Change

———

Key Points

'Change is not made without inconvenience, even from worse to better.'
RICHARD HOOKER (1554–1600), English theologian

INTRODUCTION

For most of us Hooker's bland remark quoted above will seem to be a serious understatement of our personal experience of change in two major respects. First, having sustained substantial change a number of times, as most of us have in our working environment, many will find it becomes an increasing act of faith to expect it to be 'from worse to better'. Second, the word 'inconvenience' seems laughably lightweight in the context of some of the change initiatives in which we may have been participants.

Following a decade and a half during which organizations of all kinds have undergone restructuring, right-sizing, de-layering, out-sourcing, process re-engineering, and so on (there has been no shortage of models from which the restless manager can choose), a beleaguered workforce apparently feels that things are deteriorating rather than going, as Hooker would have it, from worse to better. A survey conducted by *Management Today* in mid 1998 reported a British workforce which felt itself to be stressed, to be working longer hours than previously, expecting to have to work even longer hours, and further expecting that work will make an even greater intrusion into their private lives.

Quite separately there is an increasing body of evaluative research indicating that few change initiatives undertaken by organizations produce the results hoped and anticipated for them. Change, it seems, has got itself a bad name; it is expected to accelerate in pace, it is greeted with increasing cynicism by the workforce and it is questionably successful in outcome. This has led Harvey Robbins and Michael Finley, those cheerful Midwestern iconoclasts to write a book called *Why Change Doesn't Work – Why Initiatives Go Wrong and How To Try Again – and Succeed.* The title may not be snappy but I recommend the content.

WHY DOES CHANGE FAIL?

What is 'inconvenient' (Hooker's word, not mine) about change is that it involves unlearning and relearning. Learning, to be effective, has to be reinforced by experience. If 1+1=2 is found, in our experience always to be the case, we learn it and behave accordingly. If it is only true this quarter and may change next, or if separate sources of information offer differing views of what 1+1 might equal, then two things happen: first we are suspicious about the quality of the information; and second, we will not change behaviour to support its purported accuracy.

Ultimately organizational change depends on the human beings working in the organization changing the way they behave. In a complex system like an organization it further involves this happening in a co-ordinated way among many people all at the same time. Changed behaviour is the result of new belief systems and itself demonstrates to the 'unbelievers' the viability of the new behaviour. The trick is to establish the momentum for change in the organization, and we will return to this later in this book.

> *So to make a change initiative work in an organization, it requires that its people believe things other than they believe now, change the way they behave to support those beliefs, and, in so doing, develop a series of successful examples which generate a momentum helping others to change their behaviour.*

BELIEF AS THE PRECURSOR TO CHANGE

Strongly held beliefs have enabled the most extraordinary behaviour throughout history. A strong belief in the rectitude of Christianity enabled tens of thousands of people over three centuries to engage in the Crusades, leaving home and family, trekking across Europe and slaughtering or being slaughtered by those who did not share their belief. A strong belief in the rectitude of Islam had an equal and opposite effect.

There is plainly a correlation between the strength of the belief and the energy consumed in following it. In the case of the Crusades the avoidance of damnation or the immediate translation to paradise were incentives guaranteeing enthusiastic participation. These might be hard to replicate in a modern corporate environment. But if that was the carrot, the stick was equally powerful in soliciting compliance. It was most certainly inadvisable to decline the summons of your feudal lord to head off to the Holy Land, or resist your Sultan's requirement that you engage in war with the godless. A ticket to paradise being beyond the gift of most organizations, it is usually easier in the modern corporate environment to mimic the stick than the carrot.

What is really important is that those who enact the change really believe that it is worth their time and attention. If the purpose of the change captures their attention, engages their enthusiasm and is perceived as the right thing to do, then the chances of success increase by leaps and bounds.

The enemy to generating this kind of enthusiasm is, of course, the frequency with which change has to be enacted. If restructure, reorganization. re-engineering, etc. takes place on a regular basis, then unsurprisingly, it is dismissed as flavour-of-the-day, irrelevant to the organization, more hassle and so on. Any change initiative which comes surrounded by this kind of belief system is pretty well doomed.

CHANGE AND THE CONTEMPORARY OPERATING CLIMATE

Balanced against the problem of cynicism increasing with the frequency of change is the inescapable fact that to continue to be competitive, to continue to serve customers better, to keep up with technology, organizations do have to change more frequently, and often more radically than ever before. It has become a truism to say that the pace of change is accelerating, but unless you absorb this fact and take its implications seriously, you are unlikely to be competitive for long.

It is the pace and unpredictability of events in the operating environment which triggers the need for frequent fast change in the organization.

The modern organization is navigating in increasingly uncharted waters; things, really radically unexpected things, happen very fast and organizations need to respond rapidly at the tactical level. It is the pace and unpredictability of events in the operating environment which triggers the need for frequent fast change in the organization. Some of the key drivers of accelerating environmental change are as follows.

- *Increasingly demanding customers* – intense competition in most spheres means that customers are getting improving levels of service, enhanced quality, and a wider choice of goods and services. Product and service life cycles are falling and more niche markets are being created. To compete, an organization must be able to offer better service, quality and the ability to create or penetrate new markets.

- *Globalization* – competition is worldwide because, increasingly, customers can shop worldwide. Goods and services move very freely round the world and sources of supply have proliferated extensively. Global events, seemingly unrelated to your organization, are in fact influencing you probably more than can be imagined. A devaluation of the Thai Baht deeply affects the ability of British shoe manufacturers to supply British retailers at competitive prices. Exceptional computer programming competence in India affects employability in Silicon Valley. A Honda manufacturing investment in England means, because of the EU, that Fiat has a new competitor in its home market – the examples are endless.

- *Technology* – IT in particular is affecting how goods are made and services delivered, how organizations run themselves internally, and how they bring their goods and services to market. The Internet is changing marketing for a number of industries. Increasingly too, with the inter-linking of networks, IT extends the potential for adding value downstream from your suppliers and upstream to your customers.

- *Non IT related technologies* – these are also having a profound effect on product and markets. Biotechnology in particular is hatching previously unimagined products addressing markets in unique ways.

- *Organizational accountability* – any organization now operates in the centre of a web of responsibilities so that, besides being answerable to the law, the owners and the customers, its obligations now extend far beyond. Environmental considerations, pressure groups, professional commitments, political accountability, industry regulation and industry reputation all affect how organizations conduct themselves and the latitude they have in which to manoeuvre.

- *People* – above all the responsibility of the organization to its employees has changed. As people increasingly become the means by which organizations can differentiate their services and add value in the eyes of their customers, so the need to attract, retain and motivate employees becomes critical.

All these influences create a turbulent and unpredictable operating environment which means that organizations are constantly in a state of change, whether they like it or not.

DESIGNING THE MODERN ORGANIZATION

'A living thing is distinguished from a dead thing by the multiplicity of the changes at any moment taking place in it.' **Herbert Spencer** *(1820–1903), English philosopher,* Principles of Biology

Like any living organization then, we must be able to design and operate organizations which are in a state of constant change at many levels. Here the key word is 'constant'. We have spoken a lot about change initiatives above, and what now has to be built is an organization which is able to balance:

- continuous ongoing change at one level
- the ability to sustain major change initiatives at another level and consolidate around them fast.

Some call it the ability to balance evolution and revolution. While that sounds good, and may help you to differentiate the needs in your mind, beware of describing continuous improvement as evolution – it may sound as if it happens naturally while, to achieve it, your people will certainly be working extremely hard. You equally stand at risk of announcing revolution on too regular a basis . . .

Successful organizations seem to be well able to distinguish between these two activities, accommodate them both in the organizational environment, and to allocate accurately the differing resources each needs to be successful.

In Chapter 12, *The Responsive Organization*, we return to this subject and offer more detailed advice on what such an organization looks like.

KAIZEN'S PARTICULAR CONTRIBUTION

Kaizen is about achieving continuous improvement. While continuous improvement embraces quality enhancement in products and services, its scope extends well beyond. *Kaizen* seeks to embrace improvement in all aspects of the organization's activities from the processes and relationships it develops for taking in materials and components from its downstream suppliers, through all its internal value adding processes, to the way it interacts with its distribution systems and its final customers.

The primary executive system of *Kaizen* is the team. Good team building produces synergy which increases productivity and stimulates the development of imaginative solutions to problems of improvement.

It is important to recognise that Kaizen *is not an initiative, it is an ongoing organizational culture which, as a matter of primary focus, is dedicated to, and active in, the processes of improvement.*

Cross-functional teaming, spanning several processes within the organization, solves functional interface problems, eliminates waste and helps focus the whole organization on customer (internal or external) satisfaction.

It is important to recognize that *Kaizen* is not an initiative it is an ongoing organizational culture which, as a matter of primary focus, is dedicated to, and active in, the processes of improvement. It is about building belief systems in the organization which consistently question whether there is not a better way. It is about creating internal systems which support and reward the restless pursuit of incremental improvement.

In support of this culture, *Kaizen* relies on developing behaviour which is honest, open and trusting. It encourages problems and difficulties to be brought to the surface so that they can be attended to. It seeks, in the words of Edwards Deming, to '. . . drive out fear from the organization . . .' so that people are not punished for bringing the bad news. It probes for the clearest understanding of the customer's need; what it is, why it is important for the customer, and how best to deliver it.

A *Kaizen* culture is also a learning culture, one in which what we do is measured so that we can define improvement. It encourages teams to stop and evaluate how they are working together as well as how they are doing against their expectations. It encourages the team to pause at the end of a shift for example, to ask the questions: What went right? What went wrong? What did we learn?

> *In designing an organization that is capable of both evolution and revolution, a* Kaizen *culture will contribute enormously to the former. The key contribution being that the need for incremental improvement is largely taken care of by a systemic* Kaizen *approach which becomes ongoing rather than an often-repeated initiative.*

THE PURPOSE OF ALL CHANGE

Before we leave these introductory generalizations about change, there is an important point to be made, one to which we will consistently return in this book.

> *The purpose of organizational change is the better to implement organizational strategy.*

The long-term survival of an organization rests fundamentally on the quality of its strategy. A strategy consists of a vision of where the organization wishes to be at some time in the future. It further needs some plans for getting there, which include a description of the markets in which it will compete, the products and services with which it will compete, and the ways in which it will differentiate itself from its competitors.

This book is not about strategy, it is about change; but to explore the opportunities for change within an organization without reference to its strategy, is much like the old aphorism that . . .

> *'. . . the surgery was completely successful but unfortunately the patient died.'*

The change will always be the surgery, but the purpose of the change is to ensure the long-term survival of the organization.

If this sounds absurdly obvious it must be said that styles of organizational change do undergo cycles of popularity. It hardly seems possible, given the cost and disruption inherent in initiating major organizational change, that it is introduced for so whimsical a reason as fashion. There is ample evidence that this is sometimes the case, however, to the extent that *Fortune* magazine for example will run occasionally an article entitled **'What's on Sale at the Consultant Boutique'**. The last of these which I read reported a decline in Process Re-engineering and an increase in Visioning.

It is an essential precursor to initiating any organizational change that doing it will contribute to the organization's strategy. If the change only tangentially addresses strategy, question seriously whether this is nice-to or need-to. Need-to means that you can easily see the link between what you intend to change and the way it helps to implement the strategy.

If the answer is nice-to, ask yourself: 'Nice for whom?'

KEY POINTS

The most important points made in this chapter are as follows.

- The purpose of initiating organizational change is to contribute towards the strategic plan.
- Research seems to indicate that few change initiatives deliver the pay-off the organization sought in introducing them.

- People are demoralized and worn out by undergoing change too often.
- Unless people believe in and support the change, it is doomed to failure.
- The pace of change in the operating environment of most organizations is accelerating. This is driven by more demanding customers, globalization, technological advance, and increased organizational accountability.
- Responding to the accelerating changes in the environment means that organizations have to be able to do two things:
  - sustain continuous ongoing improvement in quality, systems and customer satisfaction – evolution
  - be able to introduce major change initiatives when needed and get them working fast – revolution.
- *Kaizen*, the philosophy of continuous improvement, helps in the first of these organizational needs by providing the means by which improvement becomes institutionalized in the organization rather than a periodic initiative which has to be undertaken.
- Beware of fashions in organizational change; it is only worth doing if it is a strategic need-to.

CHAPTER 2

Change and Strategy in the Organization

Introduction

———

Characteristics of an Organization

———

Building a Strategy

———

Strategy in Unpredictable Times

———

Integrating Strategy and Planning
to Achieve Change

———

Hoshin Kanri and *Kaizen* Operating in Tandem

———

Continuous Improvement v. Breakthrough . . . Again

———

Key Points

'I have always thought that one man of tolerable abilities may work great changes, and accomplish great affairs among mankind, if he first forms a good plan, and, cutting off all amusements or other employments that would divert his attention, make the execution of that same plan his sole study and business.'

BENJAMIN FRANKLIN (1706–90), US statesman, writer

INTRODUCTION

Having pointed out in the last chapter how difficult it is to change organizations, most of the rest of this book is about how you can set about doing it. It is to help you, in the words of Benjamin Franklin, above, '. . . form a good plan . . .' although I hope that implementing it will not mean that you have to '. . . (cut) off all amusements etc . . .'. The fact is, the better the plan, the easier will be its execution.

To help us we will develop a way of looking at the organization that enables us to deconstruct it into a number of component parts. Addressing each of these parts then enables us to develop an approach to change which might assist a planning process. At least it will provide a context for thinking about the way change can be introduced.

First of all it is important to reassert the thought we introduced at the end of the first chapter, namely that the strategy of the organization is its key to survival. Dealing essentially with the products and services it will provide and the markets to which it will provide them, the strategic plan lays out the broad canvas of how it intends to go forward. A key ingredient is the means by which it will differentiate itself from its competitors; what will it do (or have) which makes customers choose it over other providers.

Everything that the organization does must contribute to that strategy. This means that the way in which it organizes itself, the systems and processes it uses, how it trains and develops its people, and how it takes decisions must all contribute towards and support the strategy it is pursuing.

Put another way, the systems and processes of an organization must revolve around the strategy in much the same way as the planets in our solar

The systems and processes of an organization must revolve around the strategy in much the same way as the planets in our solar system revolve around a central sun.

system revolve around a central sun. If the strategy changes, then so must each of the parts of the organization.

It is important, too, to realize that the 'parts' we will look at are not physical entities as an operating division might be, rather they are characteristics of the way in which the organization works which, when we look closely at them, provide us with clues as to what we might have to change in order to support the strategy better.

CHARACTERISTICS OF AN ORGANIZATION

Diagrammatically we could represent the organization like this.

Figure 2.1   *Strategy and the organization's characteristics*

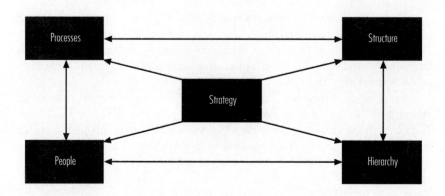

To clarify further, let us take a first look at each of these sets of characteristics so that we know what we are talking about before we start looking at them in greater detail.

Processes

These concern the way in which work flows through the organization. At its simplest, an organization takes in raw material at one end, passes it through a number of processes each of which does something which adds value. At the end a product emerges which can be sold for a price which exceeds the cost incurred in adding the value at each stage of the process. The processes the organization uses have a material effect on its cost base, hence its competitiveness. Processes also affect the quality of a product or the degree of satisfaction a customer may feel. Processes also cover workflows which have little to do with manufacture, they also embrace subjects like accounting, sales and marketing activities, and so on.

Structure

This is the way in which an organization divides the work up. In most organizations the structure is a series of functional divisions. This gives us, for example, a Design Department, which exercises the function of designing the products or service we provide. It might give us a Manufacturing Department, which exercises the function of making the product or service. It gives us an Accounting Department, and so on. While this kind of functionally based structure is most familiar, there are a number of other ways in which organizations are structured, for example, on a market-based axis. This means that an operating division in the structure provides all services (e.g. design, manufacture, accounting, etc.) for a given market while a different operating division does the same for a different market.

The way in which an organization divides up its structural components has, unsurprisingly, a huge effect on what goes on within it. It thus represents a prime consideration when one thinks of having to change it.

Hierarchy

This describes the ranks of seniority in the organization. The purpose of a hierarchy is to locate where decisions are taken in the organization, where accountability and responsibility are fixed and who supervises the work of whom. In general the bigger the hierarchy, the slower the organization is to take decisions. This means that, again a generalization, organizations are getting flatter with fewer layers of hierarchy. Besides speeding up organizational responsiveness, smaller hierarchies are usually cheaper to operate.

People

Putting people last in this list in no way implies that they are the least important component in an organizational system. Quite the reverse, in most organizations they are absolutely the most important element. We have already established that the way people behave is determined by what they believe in. This means that the organizational culture, the beliefs commonly held by the employees, enormously affects the ability to change. More importantly what people believe about their organization has a lot to do with the other major organizational characteristics we have identified above.

> *The next few chapters will look at each of these sets of organizational characteristics and assess the options each presents for change. One can look upon them as a set of change levers; what are the effects of operating each? Some will be more effective than others. Effectiveness may change depending on the sort of change intended. Collectively they pretty well embrace all the change options at the manager's disposal. Throughout this process we will also be tracking the contribution* Kaizen *makes in each area.*

To give a flavour of the potential for change in each of these groups of organizational characteristics the following table might help.

Table 2.1   *The effects of change on the organization's characteristics*

	The Upsides	The Downsides
Changes in organizational process	• Probably has the most immediate effect. • Usually manages to trim operating costs.	• Organization often 'misses a beat' as change is enacted. • Risky – you must be sure the process redesign covers all the angles. • Often leads to staff redundancy hence a demoralized workforce.
Changes in organizational structure	• Can often lead to radical and beneficial reappraisals of what is important round here. • Usually, but not always, reduces cost. • Often provides good staff developmental potential.	• Takes people time to respond to new bosses and form new relationships. • Often seen as moving the deck chairs . . .

	The Upsides	The Downsides
Changes in organizational hierarchy	• There will always be gainers and losers. • Generally eliminating hierarchy has a good effect – usually seen as democratizing. • Almost always saves costs.	• There will always be gainers and losers. People are often slow to absorb the import of different levels of accountability. • Can be expensive in the short term.
People-related changes – can be new people or new belief systems	• Changed belief systems can produce huge productivity increase. • Involving people in the change planning can generate creative solutions. • Teaming often generates higher levels of staff satisfaction. • The most enduring form of change to enact.	• Takes longer to achieve than any other avenue of change. • Takes more energy and hard work than any other avenue of change. • New people can take time to be assimilated.

BUILDING A STRATEGY

'If you know the enemy and know yourself, you need not fear the result of a hundred battles. If you know yourself but not the enemy, for every victory gained you will also suffer a defeat. If you know neither the enemy nor yourself, you will succumb in every battle.' **Sun Tzu** *(6th–5th century B.C.), Chinese General*

Strategy is literally the art of being a General. The purpose of Generals is to win wars. Strategy is not necessarily about the winning of battles (though that helps), in the end it is about winning wars, victory in the long haul. In its business context, strategy is the art of guiding the organization so that it continues to exist and triumphs over its competitors.

Strategy is the art of guiding the organization so that it continues to exist and triumphs over its competitors.

The process of building a strategy usually follows a number of steps:

- ***defining purpose*** – deciding what it is the organization is there to do. That means defining the benefits it provides for its customers and stakeholders

- ***creating a vision*** – getting clear about where we want the organization to be in the future. Visions define quantitative as well as qualitative aspirations

- ***defining the values*** – agreeing the rules by which the organization chooses to play. That means being clear about the code of conduct it will follow with all the stakeholders of the organization

- ***defining the customers or markets*** – agreeing the categories of people it is serving

- ***defining the products or services*** we will provide – that means if we are to achieve our purpose, above, how will we do it, what sorts of products and services should we develop, and how will we bring them to our customers

- ***defining our differentiation*** – how will we be different from our competitors? What will make our customers favour us over others?

The process is as much about knowing yourself as it is about knowing your competitors.

The process of building this strategy is usually lengthy and requires collecting a great deal of information, conducting detailed analyses and being imaginative. Importantly, as the quotation from Sun Tzu above makes clear, the process is as much about knowing yourself as it is about knowing your competitors.

STRATEGY IN UNPREDICTABLE TIMES

Earlier we established that the climate in which modern organizations operate is turbulent, discontinuous with the past, and it is hard to predict what is likely to happen next. We concluded that the way organizations had to respond to these conditions was to build into themselves the capacity or ability to achieve two types of change, we called them evolution – getting better at what we do, and revolution – being able to achieve breakthrough, doing things that we have never done before.

This requirement is an example of how the modern organization is increasingly compelled to look at its strategy more in terms of being clear about the capabilities it must build than in defining a plan. The strategy gurus refer to the **core competencies** of the organization; this means its intrinsic capabilities, the things that it has to be good at in order to survive. Hamel and Pralahad[1] refer to **Strategic Architecture**, by which they mean the shape and nature of the organization.

If we find it hard to write a plan that anticipates accurately what will happen and how we will respond, then the alternative is to create a strong sense of overall direction. Simultaneously we accept that plans are likely to have to change continually to accommodate a shifting operating environment.

> *Perhaps the most useful analogy comes from sailing. We must know where we are, and we must be very clear about where we want to be –* ***the Vision***. *Getting from one to the other obviously means that we will encounter fair winds that help, unfavourable winds that we have to cope with, currents which will move us off course and for which we will have to compensate –* ***the operating environment***. *All of this is feasible provided we have the right kind of boat and crew to do it –* ***the core competencies***.

Increasingly, then, organizations define strategic direction very clearly and concentrate on building the core competencies to enable the journey. Operating plans do, of course, exist but they tend to address shorter periods of time.

INTEGRATING STRATEGY AND PLANNING TO ACHIEVE CHANGE

Among the more successful systems for integrating the developing of strategy and its conversion into operations is the process known as *hoshin kanri*. The great strength it offers is the ability to align the whole organization through a strategy-cum-planning process. This act of alignment itself achieves change within the organization.

To understand *hoshin kanri* as a change system better, let us look first at the system it replaces. Classic Management by Objectives (MBO) implies that the boardroom develops a strategy that is then passed down through the various operating levels of the organization. At each level, the overall strategy is deconstructed into a set of operating objectives which are then agreed with operating units. The organization monitors its performance against those objectives on an ongoing basis.

The great advantage of the MBO system is that it creates a mechanism by which every employee is made aware of the expectations of him or her, and possibly also the context in which the objectives have been established. The disadvantage of the system is that employees work towards achieving the objectives (for which there is frequently additional reward) as an end in itself rather than as a means of delivering the purpose. If the game changes unexpectedly, a centrally controlled system like this is simply too slow to respond.

Hoshin kanri, on the other hand, attempts to create of each operating unit a strategic cell in its own right. That means that the unit, often a team, has to spend time in developing its own purpose, its own vision, and the values by which it will operate. Then it must carefully consider the products and services it will offer to its customers (whether these are internal or external customers), and the standards the customer will expect. It has also to look at the alternatives the customers might have to acquire these products and services elsewhere – the competition. A complete micro strategy if you like.

Rather than the unit or team simply being a cog in a giant corporate machine then, it is a strategic unit with clear direction and focus. Having this direction and focus enables the unit to change to reflect differences in its operating environment. The organization overall then starts to develop a far more dynamic ability to change because it no longer has to enact change centrally in response to peripheral events, rather it responds at the periphery all the time. The integrity of the response of each unit is guided by the strategy it has developed.

When this is the case, it becomes a matter of prime importance that the strategy of each unit is aligned with the organization's overall strategy. *Hoshin kanri* achieves this by a continuing process of consultation and ongoing planning. Strategic direction (as distinct from a strategic plan) emerges from the top of the company but has often itself been established by a wide consensus gathering exercise. This strategic direction really outlines the company's purpose, vision and values.

Passing this strategic direction through the organization activates the strategy building of each of the operating units. Each unit aligns its purpose with the overall strategic direction and works to develop its ability to serve its customers.

> *The focus of each unit is essentially outward, based on its customers, rather than inward, based on the implementation of a plan. It is this change of operating unit focus which ultimately enables the organization to change and adapt to its customers (externally and internally) in a more flexible, dynamic and immediate way.*

HOSHIN KANRI AND *KAIZEN* OPERATING IN TANDEM

Many organizations wrestle with the problem of implementing strategy and at the same time allowing the operating units a degree of freedom of response. The evidence is that operating units which have a high degree of autonomy over how things are to be done are significantly more productive than those which are tightly controlled from above.

The evidence is that operating units which have a high degree of autonomy over how things are to be done are significantly more productive than those which are tightly controlled from above.

Strategy implementation requires that the whole organization marches to the same beat, but the need for responsiveness and agility are best achieved by devolved decision making, the freedom, by those closest to the customer, to change the way they do things. The marriage of *Kaizen*, which is essentially a process based activity, with *hoshin kanri*, which is essentially an alignment-gaining activity, helps resolve some of this dilemma.

Let us suppose that the operating units of the organization are all *Kaizen* teams. That is they are teams with a strongly declared purpose, focused closely on customers, and working to a philosophy of continuous improvement in quality, customer service, and internal process efficiency.

Involving these *Kaizen* teams in a *hoshin kanri* planning exercise is as natural a development as one could wish for. The disciplines and skills that the *Kaizen* team has developed require only the front end, the activating event, of corporate strategic direction to position their activities appropriately within the overall organizational system. Provided that in doing this they do not lose sight of their customer, process and quality enhancement activities, they will then develop the peripheral flexibility the organization is seeking, flexibility aligned with the central strategic direction.

Figure 2.2 should help you understand the interaction of *Kaizen* and *hoshin kanri* from the perspective of a team or operating unit. In it the categories of change are defined, located and criteria established.

Figure 2.2   *The interaction of* Kaizen *and* hoshin kanri

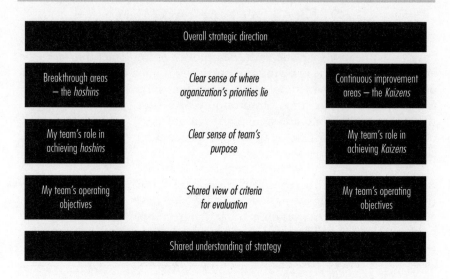

CONTINUOUS IMPROVEMENT V. BREAKTHROUGH . . . AGAIN

We suggested earlier that the modern organization required the in-built ability to achieve continuous improvement in quality, service, processes and customer satisfaction. At the same time it needed the ability to break through into the new and different.

Organizations, Hewlett Packard among them, which use *Kaizen* and *hoshin kanri* frequently (though it must be said inaccurately[2]) identify their *Kaizens* – continuous improvement activities, and distinguish them from the *hoshins*, the areas in which they are working for breakthrough.

This has a certain value, for it describes two kinds of change with which the unit is dealing: the ongoing systemic developmental type change on the one hand, contrasted with initiative-originating change. Both are usually essential to organizational strategy, realizing that they are different kinds of activities, and that one is unlikely to flow out of the other is a useful orientation for employees.

Here is a matrix that might help.

	Kaizen	Hoskins
Translates as	• '. . . good change . . .'	• 'navigation/compass . . .'
Purpose	• continuous improvement – quality, service and process	• breakthrough
Occurs because	• it is systemic within the organization	• it is initiative-directed by the strategic intent
Operates by	• incremental steps	• start-up, acquisition
Addresses	• existing products and services • existing systems and work processes	• new products/new markets • new/unique systems and work processes
Achieves	• consolidation in existing markets • competitive advantage by product/service improvement or by cost reduction	• entry into new markets • competitive advantage by being a new entrant or providing a different offer
Requires	• attention to detail • root cause analysis • problem solving • cross-functionality • gaining consensus	• innovative thinking • readiness to disrupt markets • risk taking • speed of action

KEY POINTS

What we have developed in this chapter are a number of strands relating change to strategy. Broadly they are these.

- Change is only worth doing if it supports the strategy.
- The way strategy is defined is changing, moving from a strategic plan more towards defining a strategic direction and developing the competencies and capabilities the organization needs to enable it to pursue that direction.
- A centrally imposed strategic plan supported by management by objectives is too inflexible and ponderous a means of implementing strategy.
- *Hoshin kanri* is a possible answer. It treats each operating unit as a strategic entity with its own micro strategy, developed as you would develop an organizational strategy.

- Units align themselves with the organizational strategy but essentially maintain their focus on the customers and thus respond to customer changes faster and more appropriately.

- When *hoshin kanri* is used with a *Kaizen* system, you virtually achieve two types of change: systemic ongoing improvement – the *Kaizens*, and strategy-initiated change requiring breakthrough – the *hoshins*.

Notes

1.   Hamel, G. and Pralahad, C.K. (1994) *Competing for the Future*, Harvard Business Press.

2.   'Hoshin' does not mean 'breakthrough'. Its most literal translation is 'compass' in the navigational sense.

CHAPTER 3

Change and Work Processes

'If you have great talents, industry will improve them: if you have but moderate abilities, industry will supply their deficiency.'

SIR JOSHUA REYNOLDS (1723–92), English artist

INTRODUCTION

At the beginning of the previous chapter we laid out the four major categories of organizational characteristics which we need to understand and evaluate for the potential they offer us in planning change. This chapter explores the area of work processes. The quotation above is to alert you that this avenue for change is one which usually requires detailed analyses, close observation of what goes on in the organization, and, whether you are talented or not, you will usually need 'great industry' to effect changes in work processes.

Processes usually represent a complex web of inter-dependent activities and because the organization is deeply involved with them, they represent an important area for gauging how we can enact change.

The processes the organization uses start from the point of the acquisition of materials; processes affect all its internal value-adding activities to the provision of a product or service. Processes further extend to the organization's distribution systems and its interaction with its final customer. Processes usually represent a complex web of inter-dependent activities and because the organization is deeply involved with them, they represent an important area for gauging how we can enact change.

WORK PROCESS MODELS

First let us understand what a work process is and how a number of them, some sequential, some parallel, go on to make up a total workflow through the organization. Each process has an input, within the process something is done, and as a result we have an output. This output then becomes the input to one or more processes which follow in sequence.

Hence, for example, a despatch note from the warehouse might be an input to an invoicing process. The output of this process is a document to the client, an input to data records, an input to accounting records and so on.

Here is what a single process might look like.

Figure 3.1   *A generic work process*

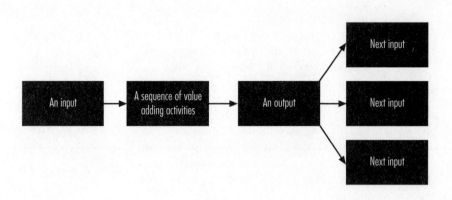

Many such processes may take place within a single operating division of the organization, and, of course, the work also flows across the borders between different operating divisions. A production line is a classic example of a workflow with each stage in the line enhancing the input it receives by the adding another component or part.

It is important to realize that while production lines are not characteristic of them, service industries too have workflows passing through them with perhaps less easily observed things happening in each process. This book for example, before it reached manufacturing stage, will have passed through a number of work processes. The first of these is the acquisition of knowledge by the author, the second is organizing the knowledge, the third is writing it and producing a manuscript. The next stage involves editing the manuscript and so on.

All the work processes described above are lateral ones. The organization also has vertical processes which operate from the top of the company downwards and upwards from the bottom. The *hoshin kanri* planning and alignment gaining activity described in the last chapter is a vertical process. Value is added to the strategic direction by each of the operating units, and the final strategy represents the total accretion of all this value.

THE TROUBLE WITH WORK PROCESSES

Over a period of time any organization develops redundant work processes. Things are done for purposes that are no longer relevant, and sometimes nobody can even remember why the organization decided to do it that way in the first place. Redundant work processes cost money; doing them occupies more time, requires more people, probably uses other resources as well, and they slow the workflow down. While it is fairly easy to identify examples of wasteful or sub-optimal work practices within an organization, it is a lot more difficult to cut them out.

Redundant work processes cost money; doing them occupies more time, requires more people, probably uses other resources as well, and they slow the workflow down.

This has led to the rise of business process re-engineering (BPR), an activity that sets out to eliminate all non-value-adding processes from the organization's workflows. In practice BPR is usually embarked upon as a precursor to cutting operating costs and for this reason it has got itself a bad name and seems to have passed its zenith of popularity.

Perhaps one of the reasons is that BPR is generally regarded as too traumatic for the organization, often causing greater problems than those it set out to solve. It is most often introduced as a new change initiative within the organization, a team is put together, often with the help of external consultants, to work through all the major work flows to simplify, streamline and re-engineer. For many organizations this has seemed like the grim reaper scything its way through well established practices and leaving a wake of redundant people behind it.

> *Unquestionably organizations cannot afford to sustain wasteful, expensive or inappropriate work processes. The need to change those practices depends, however, on the degree to which they support or frustrate the implementation of the organization's strategy.*

WHAT *KAIZEN* CAN OFFER

The primary contribution *Kaizen* makes to the organization's ability to optimize work processes is to deal with improvement as an ongoing practice. *Kaizen* espouses continuous improvement, and this embraces processes as well as considerations of quality. In fact *Kaizen* looks at

The primary contribution Kaizen makes to the organization's ability to optimize work processes is to deal with improvement as an ongoing practice.

process as part of quality, and quality as part of process.

The organization which can rely on continuous attention to process improvement need not spend its energy in high profile initiatives which are seen by the staff as threatening. If part of the organizational culture is the conviction that continuous improvement is possible, and this is backed by credible practices to achieve it, then the need to scare the organization evaporates.

Let us run through some of the core concepts of *Kaizen* to get a view of how they affect work processes in organizations.

Table 3.1 *How the core concepts of* Kaizen *change work processes*

Concept	Meaning	How it changes work processes
The production cell	This usually means a team of people responsible for producing a given group of products.	*Kaizen* approaches assure that all the resources necessary for doing the job are clustered together within the production cell.
	It is different from a production line which is engaged in a series of sequential enhancements, with responsibility only for the individual process.	This differs from the more usual technique of grouping resources by function. In manufacturing this might mean lathes in one department, milling machines in another. In a service environment it might mean, say, passing a customer enquiry from Despatch to Accounting and so on.
	Framed originally in a manufacturing context, it can as easily apply to the reception desk of an hotel, or the customer services unit of a bank for example.	Not only must the resources be to hand, they must be under the control of the production cell.
Gemba	The 'real place'; the 'coal-face'; the place where the work happens.	*Kaizen* locates the responsibility and the expectation of process improvement with those who are actually involved with the process.

Concept	Meaning	How it changes work processes
	The operating entity – usually a team, but could be members of a department.	This responsibility extends from recognition of problems, diagnosis, root cause analysis (finding out what lies behind the problem), and fixing it.
	The place where the value is added. The Manager's Desk is emphatically NOT *gemba*.	*Gemba* implies closeness to the client (internal or external); frequently the scope of solution involves the client's participation.
Five Ss of housekeeping – describing the working environment of the production cell	*Seiri* – getting rid of materials you don't need.	Creates optimum conditions for the work processes to take place.
	Seiton – placing materials and resources for easy accessibility.	Saves time and energy and hence improves the team's productivity.
	Seiso – keeping the work areas scrupulously clean.	Applies the same principles of tidiness and cleanup to things like database maintenance, record keeping, etc.
	Seiketsu – scheduling regular cleaning up and clearing out operations.	Part of the thinking to support *muda* – see below
	Shitsuke – making all the above regular tasks meet agreed standards at agreed intervals. Don't just do it when things get in a mess.	
JIT and *kanban*	Just in Time '*Kanban*' means a card or a ticket. It is used to represent the idea of the inventory card showing when new supplies are needed. The thinking here is that inventory (components, in a manufacturing environment) are delivered to *gemba* precisely when they are needed and hence the labour and cost of storage are reduced.	Getting materials to the point they are needed just when they are needed allows the process to operate at a steady pace uninterrupted by shortage or multiple handling. JIT, when extended down a value chain back from the process to the point of origination, and up the value chain from the process to the point of delivery, is complex but the pay-off in storage space, inventory investment and multiple handling is usually huge.

Concept	Meaning	How it changes work processes
JIT and *kanban* (continued)		Across a total organization effective JIT will have an effect on product break-even, potentially on margins, and ultimately on the whole overhead and investment profile.
		Effective JIT also responds to flexibility of demand, the system accelerating if demand rises and slowing down if it falls off. This equalizes economic fluctuation across the
Muda	Means 'waste' and the aim, of course, is the elimination of waste.	value system.
		Kaizen implies ongoing and committed reduction of waste.
		This means that the production cell sets itself the task of eliminating the unproductive. It means looking for better ways, eliminating redundant processes or parts of processes, ensuring that the system is as lean as possible.
		You can readily see that the Five Ss, JIT and *kanban* are all techniques by which the concept of *muda* can be eliminated.
		Ultimately this delivers the concept of 'lean production'. The stress on the word 'production' arises because much of *Kaizen* developed within manufacturing environments.
		The concept has equal value, though perhaps less transparency in service based environments.
Poke-yoka	Designing something that is fail-safe.	While primarily a technique developed for the assembly

Concept	Meaning	How it changes work processes
	A component which fits only one way so that it cannot be installed incorrectly	line, the idea of designing the foolproof can contribute enormously to productivity by preventing reworking following quality inspection – indeed by eliminating the need for inspection.
		In system terms it can be useful by minimizing error and, for example in the use of software, it protects against data corruption.
Set-up time reduction	Reducing the amount of time taken in changing machinery over from one product to another.	Again essentially a manufacturing application but the thinking behind it is important.
		To achieve a fast change-over the processes involved must be simple and easy to learn.
		Designing systems and procedures which are transparent and simple inherently increases productivity by lack of down time, but it also raises the flexibility of the production cell if the expertise required for the change-over can be readily learned.
Total productive maintenance	Routine preventive maintenance of equipment so that it fails less frequently.	If the machines go down, so does productivity, so keeping machines in good working order ensures that the processes they support continue without interruption.
		In general this simply implies taking care of equipment rather than turning employees into service engineers.

Case Study

Wai-Kwok Lo, Managing Director of Computer Products Asia Pacific Ltd in Hong Kong reports in *The TQM Magazine* No. 5 1997 an interesting case of the implementation of Deming's[2] principles of Total Quality Management. From that article (which is well worth reading in its entirety) we look at those aspects which particularly deal with work processes.

The company produces some 5 million power conversion units per year, these are AC/DC converters and switching supplies. It has a most successful record, having won several awards for quality and for productivity. The company is also certified ISO 9001.

Working with its component suppliers, the company instituted a ship-to-stock programme. The purpose was to minimize incoming inspection. Potential vendors were subject to formal evaluation of their ability to provide consistently low-defect products which met specified requirements. Vendor selection was not based on price but on the concept of total cost – i.e. the cost of the product throughout its life cycle.

These vendor management processes also appear to have enabled the introduction of JIT and also increased flexibility in manufacturing capacity.

At the same time the company focused itself on constant, ongoing improvement of the systems of production. It implemented a process of 'corrective action'. This implied that the company formally investigated all instances of nonconformity, analyzed all possible contributory factors and recommended corrective action. It then reviewed the effect of the corrective action it had taken and finally recorded procedural changes that resulted. The reader might find this description a practical example of what we have referred to earlier as root cause analysis.

Next the company moved to address a number initiatives which it describes as requiring 'overall optimization'. This involved creating cross-functional teams that designed umbrella-type processes to control and make sense of the differing aspirations of functional departments within the organization. Previously manufacturing departments had been rated on reducing unit costs but this was leading to longer production runs and a consequent increase in inventory. Optimization of the processes involved required substituting measures which operated in tandem, unit cost on the one hand, balanced with inventory turn on the other. This led to the formation of SIP (sales, inventory and operations planning) initiative.

Other cross-functional process initiatives were introduced into the organization beside the cost/inventory one mentioned above. These covered asset management, and quality improvement.

This focus on the processes of the company, linked to the philosophy of continuous improvement have enabled the company to sustain massive sales increase, continuous cost reduction averaging 7 per cent per year and a declining rate of defects in outgoing goods.

In summary then *Kaizen* offers us two extraordinarily powerful streams of assistance in the area of optimizing processes:

- an ongoing culture of process re-engineering rather than an initiative-driven apocalypse
- a large number of tools and disciplines which facilitate continuous process improvement, quality enhancement and increasing customer satisfaction.

Kaizen practitioners are compelled by the simplicity and clarity of its concepts. Phrases like 'common-sense', 'using your brain', etc. pepper conversations with them. Masaaki Imai, one of the gurus of *Kaizen* holds the view that applying common sense to the use of existing systems and technology can often achieve better results than substantial reinvestment.

An interesting observation by Mr Wai-Kwok Lo contrasts Deming's approach to TQM with the more modern approach of Hammer, of Process Re-engineering fame. The difference in his eyes rests in Deming's focus on the human aspects of substantial change processes.

KEY POINTS

The main points covered in this chapter are as follows.

- Changing work processes usually require a lot of analysis and hard work.
- Conversely changing processes pretty well immediately change the behaviour of people.
- Every work process has an input, a sequence of value adding activities and an output.
- Work processes operate laterally within the organization (e.g. raw material to finished product) and vertically (e.g. the planning processes an organization uses).
- Over time the work processes of all organizations develop elements of redundancy and waste.
- Most organizations simply cannot afford to maintain sub-optimal work processes.
- Process re-engineering, the invention of which is credited to Michael Hammer, is one way of improving work processes by eliminating all non value adding activities.
- Process re-engineering has developed the reputation of being the precursor to employee redundancy.
- *Kaizen* offers two major avenues for improving work processes:
  - first, it is an ongoing process (as distinct from an initiative such as process re-engineering)
  - second, it provides a number of tools which when applied really help transform work processes.
- Key *Kaizen* tools to effect changes in work processes are:
  - the use of the production cell, i.e. a team with total responsibility for production
  - *gemba*, constituting such teams from the people who have the greatest experience
  - the Five Ss of housekeeping, creating the best possible environment for value to be added
  - JIT and *kanban*, eliminating handling and storing of components to save time and money and to allow processes to operate at a steady pace
  - *muda*, the rigorous and ongoing pursuit of eliminating waste

- *poke-yoka*, designing fail-safe error reducing processes and components
- set-up time reduction, making it easy for the production cell to shift from one set of activities to another
- total productive maintenance, looking after machines so that down-time is minimized.

- *Kaizen* practitioners demystify its processes and talk of it as being common sense management and simply using your brain.

Note

1. W. Edwards Deming was the architect of the renaissance of Japanese manufacturing after the Second World War. Many of the core concepts of *Kaizen*, continuous improvement, and quality management owe their existence to him.

CHAPTER 4

Change and Organizational Structure

'Form and function are a unity, two sides of one coin. In order to enhance function, appropriate form must exist or be created.'

IDA P. ROLF (1896–1979), US biochemist

INTRODUCTION

When we introduced structure as one of the main available levers of change we described it as the way the organization divides up the work. If the work processes we discussed in the last chapter constitute an overall work flow, just how is that flow channelled through the organization? Through what operating departments or divisions does it pass, and what does each of those divisions do as the workflow passes through its area of responsibility? These component parts or divisions of the organization constitute its structure.

Our quotation above, originating from a biochemist, is no less true of the organization than it is in biology. The function of the organization, what is does, is dictated by its strategy. Its form, the structure, must be such as to enable and facilitate that strategy.

The structure of the organization affects a number of things, the following among them.

- The **cost of operating** – if the product or service being provided calls for multiple activities or work processes to take place then the structure is likely to be more complex and hence expensive to operate. This is especially true if the processes are very different in nature requiring high and differing levels of skill to be applied at different stages.

  The more complex the structure, the slower the company is likely to be in channelling its work flows.

- **The speed with which it does things** – again, the more complex the structure, the slower the company is likely to be in channelling its work flows.

- **The way it meets its customers' needs** – large complex structures, highly supervised, are sometimes necessary in order to protect the customer well. This is especially true in areas like health and safety where a significant part of the organization's responsibility is to ensure the customer's safety.

- **The way people behave** – all structures tend to promote an element of internal competition; this can be for resources, it can be performance rivalry. Structure affects organizational politics and the way people think, feel and hence behave.

CONTEMPORARY TRENDS IN THE STRUCTURE OF ORGANIZATIONS

The contemporary tendency in structure is to make organizations as simple, flat and transparent as possible. While large vertically integrated organizations were characteristic of early structures, modern thinking tends to favour smaller, more tightly focused operating units which are more responsive to their customers. Companies continue to get bigger but operating units tend to get smaller.

Part of the vogue for structural change in the past few years has been the drive to outsource non-core activities. Former operating units of integrated companies have been spun off to become separate entities. By and large this has been successful, but it means that many organizations are now quite complex webs or networks, some parts of which are structural components of the organization, some external providers, partners, or participants in alliances. Some of the relationships in these networks are permanent, some temporary, associated perhaps with a single project, or a particular customer requirement.

A larger number of more autonomous units, though harder to manage centrally, are collectively more effective in delivering customer satisfaction and in their speed of tactical response to the competitive environment.

What lies behind this move from vertical integration to the 'networked' organization is that a larger number of more autonomous units, though harder to manage centrally, are collectively more effective in delivering customer satisfaction and in their speed of tactical response to the competitive environment.

WHAT ARE THE OPTIONS FOR ORGANIZATIONAL STRUCTURE?

There are four basic structural options for an organization:

- functional structures
- product based structures
- market based structures
- hybrid structures which use bits and pieces of each of the above conventions side by side but attempt to address the limitations of each.

In order to understand the potential for change which each of these structural conventions offers we need briefly to examine them.

Functional structure

Despite the changes described above the functional structure remains the most common form of structure. In it the areas of functional expertise of the organization are defined and each represents a structural operating unit through which the work flows. Such a structure might look like Fig. 4.1 below.

Figure 4.1   *Example of a functional structure*

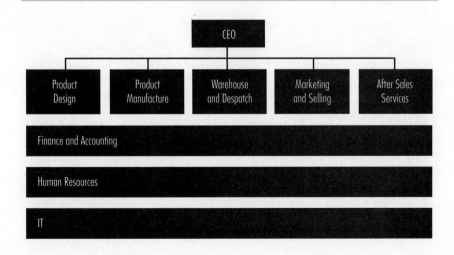

Organizations with a relatively homogeneous product line supplied to a relatively constant distribution system generally find functional structures suitable for their purposes.

The rationale behind this form of structure is that each of the separate functional units develops expertise in a particular area. Some of this expertise (Finance and Accounting, HR and IT in the example) is applied across the whole organization. Some of it (Design, Manufacture, etc. in the example) is applied at very specific stages in the process of bringing a product to a market.

Organizations with a relatively homogeneous product line supplied to a relatively constant distribution system generally find functional structures suitable for their purposes.

Functional structures offer a number of advantages.

- People in each operating unit have similar specialist interest, understand each other and communicate well.

- Functional competence means efficiency and effectiveness, sometimes economy.

- The unit can sometimes develop high expertise which can be a differentiator for the organization.

There are also some disadvantages.

- Sometimes units do not co-operate well, there can be war at the interfaces.

- Company-wide decisions are sometimes hard to implement since different units have different agendas and decisions have to be sold and resold.

- Unproductive competition for resources can develop.

- Sometimes functional expertise becomes over-engineered for the needs of the organization.

- Accountability can sometimes be hard to fix – '. . . we designed the thing brilliantly; they didn't manufacture it very well . . .'

The demolition of functionally based structures is perhaps the most common of the large change initiatives which organizations are undertaking. A condition called the 'silo effect' arises where each of the functional units defends its turf and expertise without regard to the organization's overall need. This must be addressed to cut operating cost and refocus the organization on what is really important, the customer, rather than the expertise of the operating division.

Product based structures

Here the structural components of the organization are organized round products or categories of products. Here the operating unit contains all the functional competencies needed to support the product, e.g. design, manufacture, sales and marketing, accounting, IT, etc. Graphically an organization operating a product based structure might look like Fig. 4.2 below:

Figure 4.2 *Example of a product based structure*

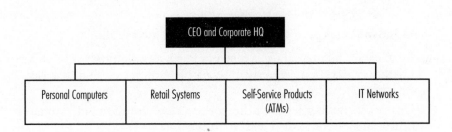

This is a simplified version of the Siemens/Nixdorf structure. Each of the main operating units is organized around a specific category of products. Each, of course, also serves different categories of markets, though it is perfectly possible that a customer might be supplied by two separate operating units. A major retailer, for example, might buy retail systems, essentially driven by scanning technology, and PCs which it might use for its general office IT.

In such a configuration the head office might also have certain operating divisions which embrace the entire company. Human Resources is a common example. In this sort of structure the head office HR function would decide policy and the operating units would implement the policy but run their individual HR functions in an aligned but autonomous manner.

Organizations whose products require rapid development, which are changed and updated often, and where the product has a short life cycle tend to favour product based structures. It also suits organizations whose products need to undergo a high degree of versioning or customer-specific modification.

In essence the focus of the unit is on maximizing the sales and development of the product and this will cause quite different behaviour among its members than if, as in a functionally based

> *system, the unit's focus is specifically on, say, design or on manufacture. It is quite easy to see that if one instituted a change in the organizational structure from functionally based structure to product based structures, the changes would be radical and would almost certainly take some time for people to un-learn functional type behaviour and re-learn product type behaviour.*

The **advantages** of product based structures are:

- swift response to competitive changes in the product
- development opportunities for members of units because each unit is a mini business offering varied functions
- the organization can fix accountability.

The **disadvantages** of product based structures are as follows.

- Smaller product based units may not be able to support the sophisticated functional expertise available in functionally based structures.
- Customers buying several different products from the same organization may have to deal with multiple units.
- Sometimes the unit reinvents the wheel rather than sharing expertise and resources among several units in the same company.
- Passionate involvement with the product sometimes blinds the unit to evidence of its decline.

Market based structures

The structural components here are focused on serving specified markets, often with a range of products and services. This kind of structure is increasingly common because highly demanding customers have come to expect their suppliers to have expertise about their needs. High technology suppliers of both hardware and software increasingly differentiate the organizations to serve, say, the financial sector, the manufacturing sector, utilities and so on.

Diagrammatically the structure looks like Fig. 4.3 opposite.

This is the organizational structure of a training company which supplies a range of training and development programmes. The rationale behind the organization is that the training or development needs of individual industry sectors change all the time, hence a selling and programme delivery system alert to those changes must exist. At the same time the way that, say, an Account Management selling

Figure 4.3   *Example of a market based structure*

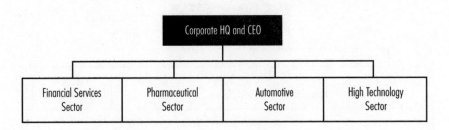

programme would need to be taught to a financial services audience is quite different from the way it would be taught to a pharmaceutical company's selling force.

In general this sort of structure suits organizations whose products or services have a wide variety of potential application but which need a high degree of client knowledge to tailor the product to meet client need. Such organizations are usually looking to achieve market share for marginally adapted products and services in specific sectors.

The **advantages** of market based structures are that they:

- produce longer term supplier/client relationships (increasing the switching cost for the client)
- focus on clients which is, increasingly, a survival issue
- improve the organization's ability to differentiate itself in a meaningful way from other suppliers.

The **disadvantages** of market based structures are that:

- the organization becomes harder to control and harmonize – units spawn *ad hoc* and often expensive processes to meet client/market needs
- units which focus on different segments tend to compete aggressively for organizational resources
- loss of key clients can create organizational vulnerability.

Hybrid structures

It is clear that each of the structural options outlined above has advantages and disadvantages. Hybrid structures choose the most appropriate of the options and then seek to minimize the disadvantages inherent in

Figure 4.4 *Example of a hybrid structure*

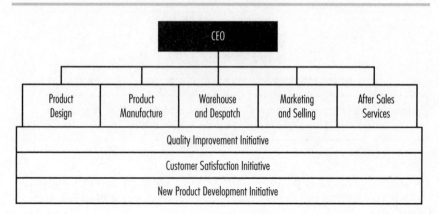

the choice by introducing what is usually a compensating set of initiatives or processes.

Figure 4.4 shows what it might look like diagrammatically when a process directed initiative is bolted onto a functional structure to create a hybrid.

In Fig. 4.4 above we have used the word initiative advisedly. When such cross-pinning of structural components is implemented, it is usually in response to a strategic need, which the present structure is not facilitating or, at worst, frustrating. Organizations usually introduce these structural components to change things; sometimes they are temporary and sometimes permanent.

Hybrid structures are often set up by introducing cross-functional teams. Members of the key operating departments (functional, in this case) are assigned to the team so that the interests of that department can be represented within the broader context of, say, Customer Satisfaction.

The **advantages** of hybrid/team based structures are as follows.

- Teams which operate synergistically can produce a high degree of positive and innovative change.

- Members of these teams represent existing departmental interests. This means that the changes they bring about are well thought through and practical to implement.

- Involving people in this kind of activity broadens their experience and adds to their development.

The **disadvantages** of hybrid/team based structures are that:

- teams can take a lot of time to come together and to develop synergy
- the teams can take a lot of management time to maintain their morale and the momentum they generate
- sometimes members of teams experience divided loyalties between the interests of their operating units and the tasking of the team.

So what . . .?

Understanding the structural options open to an organization and the upsides and downsides of each starts to provide a spectrum of the opportunities you have for using structure as a change lever. Changing the structure will not, of itself, provide a sufficient or reliable impetus to change. What does affect the behaviour of people is change in the focus, purpose and objectives inherent in a structural change.

Changing the structure will not, of itself, provide a sufficient or reliable impetus to change. What does affect the behaviour of people is change in the focus, purpose and objectives inherent in a structural change.

The table overleaf shows just how different the employees' focus, their perceived purpose and their typical objectives are in each of the types of structure.

Omitted from this matrix is, of course, the hybrid structure. This is because the hybrid structure allows you to correct the inherent imbalance of any of the structural options, usually by the use of cross-functional teams.

A moment looking at the objectives in the third column will very soon bring you to the conclusion that the effective organization cannot cleave to one set of objectives only, it must balance its objectives in a way specific to its own nature; hybrid structures enable this.

Some organizations are employing the concept of the balanced scorecard, the invention of Kaplan and Norton.[1] This requires that whole organization, and each of its structural components defines its objectives in four main areas:

- financial (or quantitative) criteria
- internal business process objectives
- customer objectives
- objectives in the area of learning and personal development needed to sustain the unit.

Type of structure	Employee focus and perceived purpose	Typical objectives
Functional	**Focus** Inward, on the function, getting it right, improving the function **Purpose** To ensure that your specific functional expertise adds value to the product/service.	**Design** • Utility/fitness for purpose/style **Manufacture** • Cost, quality of product, waste **Warehouse and Despatch** • Speed of turnaround/ accuracy **Marketing and Selling** • Revenue/market share/ customer acquisition and retention **After Sales** • Call out time/cost/fix right first time
Product based	**Focus** Outwards – competitor products '. . . building a better mousetrap . . .' **Purpose** To achieve product dominance in the prime market and, probably, penetration of all other markets.	• Unit sales/unit margins/ revenue • Achieve a differentiated product better/cheaper or different • Quality – continuous improvement • Product to market cycle time • Product life cycle extension
Market based	**Focus** Outward – on the customer – on the competitors **Purpose** Customer satisfaction, customer repeat purchase, customer retention.	• Market share/revenue • Accessibility/distribution • Customer satisfaction indices • Versioning/tailoring capability • Market extension

In general this practice meshes well with contemporary thinking that change is fastest and most effectively achieved by defining new and different objectives rather than by instituting change initiatives and processes. This thinking, popularized by Schaffer and Thomson,[2] takes the view that involving members of the work unit in the predication of demanding outcomes initiates and accelerates change faster than any considered change process currently in use. Schaffer and Thomson's experience is that when involved in defining these objectives employees will habitually set more demanding objectives than their managers would dare.

HOW *KAIZEN* CONTRIBUTES

The principles of *Kaizen* can apply in any structural configuration.

- Within a work unit the twin philosophies of continuous incremental improvement and customer focus will enhance the unit's function, theoretically delivering services of improving quality at optimal cost.

- In a cross-functional environment *Kaizen* really delivers value for the organization in that the processes teams use to achieve synergy are enormously enhanced by *Kaizen*'s focus on honesty, openness to suggestion, mutual trust and constructive confrontation.

Among the significant organizational benefits a *Kaizen* philosophy will contribute is the continuity of the values of continual improvement, customer focus, external and internal. Many organizations embark with enthusiasm on, say, a customer satisfaction programme, spending time, energy and organizational resource in the pursuit of the initiative. All too often a new planning cycle will produce another set of initiatives which are now placed centre stage.

It is this inconstancy of intention that produces the flavour-of-the-month cynicism in employees which virtually guarantees that the new initiative will run into the sand. On the other hand *Kaizen* offers the potential for building quality improvement and customer focus into the fabric of the organization's operating systems. Such organizations are far less vulnerable to employee cynicism and are at least supporting the principal success factors of all organizations.

A review of the ten key principles[3] of *Kaizen* will help illuminate how good a lubricant a *Kaizen* culture provides to the grinding gear changes of structural change.

The Ten Key Principles of Kaizen

- Focus on customers
- Make improvements unceasingly
- Acknowledge problems openly
- Promote openness
- Create work teams
- Manage projects cross functionally
- Nurture supportive relationship processes
- Develop self-discipline
- Inform every employee
- Enable every employee

Before leaving the subject of change initiated or supported through structural means, let us look at two case studies. Both are reported by Muzyka *et al.* in the *European Management Journal.*[4]

Case Study 1

Kolb and Schule is a well-established German textile manufacturer established in 1760. By 1990, although the company's revenue exceeded DM 100 million, its profits were minimal. A new managing director undertook the restructuring of the organization.

This is what they did . . .	. . . described in the terminology we have used
Introduced a new computer system	Changed work processes (see previous chapter)
Closed major production facilities, moving those they needed to cheaper manufacturing environments	Outsourced non core activities . . . . . . focused on core competencies
Developed three major operating units run as separate companies:	Moved from a functional structure to a product directed structure . . .

- soft furnishings and upholstery – also acquired a competitor in this field allowing it to address the high end of the market.
- acquired a table fashion company.
- acquired a clothing manufacturer specializing in men's clothing.

Strengthened its position in chosen product opportunity areas (by acquisition) in pursuit of market share.

As a result of these moves the company's dividend has increased twelvefold and its share value appreciated in price by 400 per cent.

Case Study 2

Trinkhaus and Burkhardt is an old and well-established private bank. It is capitalized at DM 15 billion and operates in Germany, Switzerland and Luxembourg. The far reaching financial restructuring of the 1970s when a number of countries enacted deregulation legislation led to a substantial change in banking in Europe. At the same time the bank was acquired by Midland/ HSBC, the largest banking group in the world.

This is what they did . . .	. . . described in the terminology we have used
Segmented itself into three units each targeted at clearly defined groups of customers as follows: • corporate customers – companies with more than DM 80 million turnover which were globally active and potentially needed more than one product from the bank • private customers – high net worth • investment banking.	Restructured on a customer directed basis
Created small, profit-orientated teams of specialists targeted on managing customer relationships – relationship banking.	Augmented the structural rebuild with teams whose primary responsibility was to get closer to the customer, consistently improve

Installed a new information and control system which speeded up operations.

products and services and achieve customer satisfaction.
Improved work processes – see previous chapter.

As a result the bank has grown steadily and won the Warrant Bank of the Year award. It is known for imaginative and innovative products.

Note

Trinkhaus and Burkhardt also took other steps which we shall explore in later chapters in this book:

- they reduced the number of layers in the organizational hierarchy to three
- they mandated an internal training programme for employees (85 hours per year).

KEY POINTS

- The structure of an organization (its form) must be designed to support its strategy (the organization's function).
- Altering the way a company is structured presents a number of opportunities to effect change.
- There are three structural conventions:
  - functionally based
  - product based
  - market or customer based
  - and a fourth, the hybrid structure.
- Each structure has certain strengths and certain shortcomings. The use of cross-functional teams (a hybrid structure) allows one to compensate for the shortcomings of each of the structures.
- Changing the structure, of itself, achieves nothing – the focus, purpose and objectives of the operating units must be re-established if the change is to work.

- *Kaizen* can flourish in any of the structural configurations, but it is especially effective in cross-functional teaming applications.
- *Kaizen* behaviours – the ten key principles – are of great help in managing the disruption which inevitably results from major structural change.

Notes

1.   Kaplan, R.S. and Norton, D.P. (1996) *The Balanced Scorecard,* HBS Press.

2.   Schaffer, R.H. and Thomson, H.A. (1998) *Successful Change Programmes begin with Results,* Harvard Business Review On Change.

3.   Taken from Wellington, P. (1995) Kaizen *Strategies for Customer Care,* Pitman.

4.   Muyzika, Breuninger and Rossell (1997) 'The Secret of New Growth in Old German "Mittelstand" Companies', *European Management Journal,* 15 (2).

CHAPTER 5

Change and Organizational Hierarchies

Pecking Order – '*The social hierarchy in a flock of domestic fowl in which each bird pecks subordinate birds and submits to being pecked by dominant birds.*'

American Heritage Dictionary definition

INTRODUCTION

The third of the major levers that can be operated to achieve change is altering the hierarchy of the organization. The sense in which we use the term hierarchy means the ranks of seniority in the organization. The purpose of a hierarchy is to locate where decisions are taken in the organization, where accountability and responsibility are fixed and who supervises the work of whom. Sometimes called the pecking order, the whole idea of hierarchy stems from the belief that people need an authority structure, a social framework, and a defined set of relationships in order to operate effectively.

Sometimes called the pecking order, the whole idea of hierarchy stems from the belief that people need an authority structure, a social framework, and a defined set of relationships in order to operate effectively.

Machine model

The model of the organization which has been used for the better part of the twentieth century essentially equated with a machine. Characteristics of it are:

- top down goal setting
- each employee reporting to a single superior in the hierarchy
- vertical channels of communication, predominantly top down
- position power – position in the hierarchy designating the amount of power exercised
- each manager having a defined span of control.

That model is alive and well but is increasingly seen as inappropriate to the optimal operation of the modern organization. Levels in the hierarchy have become fewer because technology has enabled faster, more accurate communication within the organization. Drucker describes the message as losing half its meaning and gaining twice the 'noise' at each level it is repeated; now the message from the chairman can be instantaneously and accurately broadcast throughout the organization in real time.

Perhaps more importantly, employees simply do not accept the quiescent, uncritical role that the hierarchical, machine model of the organization requires for it to be effective. The job-for-life in return for acceptance of the hierarchy's control is no longer part of the employer / employee contract.

Devolved organization model

The excision of layers of hierarchy from organizations – over 2 million managerial, white collar jobs are reputed to have disappeared in America during the 1990s – means that decision making has perforce been moved down the organization. It may be in part a rationalization of the cost savings achieved by delayering, or it may actually be true that decision making should be located as close as possible to the coalface; in any event, that is the commonly held wisdom.

Switching an organization's focus from the rule book, the procedures manual, to a values and strategy based response is no easy matter, but it is a means of activating radical change.

Lending credence to the philosophy of devolved decision making is the perceived need for organizations to be able to respond to events more swiftly than they did before. The more levels there are in the hierarchy, the greater the number of filters decisions will have to go through and hence the slower the response.

This devolved organization model differs radically from the machine model. In the latter employees were expected to behave predictably and within defined parameters in response to any given situation – the procedures manuals provide these definitions. In the devolved model employees are expected to behave in a manner which is consistent with the strategy of the organization, the purpose of the department in which they are operating and in accordance with the overall values of the organization.

Switching an organization's focus from the rule book, the procedures manual, to a values and strategy based response is no easy matter, but it is a means of activating radical change. The unlearning/relearning activities which have to take place usually take quite a bit of time. Errors and mistakes occur, and if the change is to be reinforced, these errors must be forgiven, the reasons for them examined and feedback given to the perpetrator. Unhappily, in most organizations the first response to such an error is to spawn another five procedures, thus vitiating any advance in devolved decision making which may have been achieved.

WHAT CHANGES IN HIERARCHY LOOK LIKE

Effecting change through relocating decision making requires a lot of planning because the change must be defined in two broad categories:

- the nature of the decisions that can be taken
- the order (size, amount of money, degree of commitment, etc.) of decision that may be taken.

To understand the implications of altering the hierarchy one should start by looking at the way the usual organizational hierarchy operates. The chart below may not reflect exactly the practice in your own organization, but it is a reasonably robust generic picture. If yours differs radically, try compiling a chart like it – use the same axes insofar as they exist and then look at the opportunities for and consequences of changing it.

Nomenclature varies greatly from one organization to another but in most, four levels of hierarchy exist below the chief executive. It is the two lowest levels of employees that are most usually merged into one in the modern organization. In some organizations both senior manager and line manager categories have been eliminated, but this is rare.

The implications of excising one or more layers of hierarchy from the organization are broadly summarized in Table 5.1. Put another way, if you alter the hierarchy you must redefine not only the reporting line but also the **focus and content** of the work. Equally you must deal with issues of **accountability** and **authority**.

You must also help the new hierarchy to visualize what success will look like and to set the objectives the unit will achieve and the metrics by which it will be judged.

As if this were not enough of a redesign commitment, these redefinitions must exist for each and every level in the hierarchy because they will all be affected by it.

Table 5.1 *A generic organizational hierarchy*

	Top Team	Senior Managers/ Managers	Line Managers/ Supervisors	Workers
Reports to	Chief Executive	Members of Top Team	Senior Managers	Managers/ Supervisors
Focus of work	Strategic – long range	Implementing strategy, long range planning and tactical response	Implementing the planning and tactical response	Getting through it day by day
Content of work	Creating competitive advantage	Implementing competitive advantage and monitoring	Supervising and improving processes	Operating and improving processes
Accountable for . . .	Whole organization	Division	Work unit	Day to day work
Authority to commit	Defined areas and defined sums of money	Defined sums of money within the division	Within the unit's budget	As agreed with Manager/ Supervisor
Success looks like	Growth, profitability, increase in shareholder value	Culture of TQM, customer satisfaction, excellence	Falling costs, improving quality, higher customer satisfaction	Easier processes, simpler operations

> In Chapter 2 we spoke of hoshin kanri, *the planning methodology by which everybody participates in strategy formulation and in strategic planning. In eliminating organizational layers, some organizations have found that the quality and integrity of decision making which takes place at all levels is greatly enhanced by the alignment achieved by this kind of participative planning.*

WHAT *KAIZEN* HAS TO OFFER

Kaizen practice, at its most effective, concentrates its energies in columns 4 and 5 of Table 5.1, i.e. in the line managers/supervisors and workers interface. In Chapter 3 we outlined the concept of *gemba* – the 'real place', the place where the work actually takes place. Successful *Kaizen*, with its strong focus on work processes, seeks to improve what goes on there and this means that the responsibilities, accountabilities and visions of success at this level in the organization are very clearly defined.

Typically the supervisor, who may also be called the foreman, or the team leader, is responsible for quality, cost and delivery – *Kaizen's* famous QCD – of whatever the work unit puts out. In a manufacturing environment this will be a semi-finished or finished product. It could as easily be a sub-edited manuscript, or a written proposal to a client. Importantly the supervisor is not simply managing the production of the thing that is put out, but its QCD as well.

You might suggest that this is perfectly obvious, but what makes the difference in *Kaizen* is the underlying expectation that the quality will continuously improve, the cost will continually fall and the delivery time will continuously improve. Our *Kaizen* supervisor's responsibilities then also embrace maintaining current standards on the one hand and improving them on the other. Maintaining what goes on in the work unit is extremely important. If the processes being used are not maintained they will deteriorate. Equally if they are not subject to the scrutiny of seeking continuous improvement, they will remain static.

To achieve the QCD output the *Kaizen* supervisor manages the five Ms (*Kaizen* crawls with mnemonics based on initial letters) these are **m**anpower, **m**aterials, **m**achines, **m**ethods and **m**easurements. Though devised for the production line, the concept of the five Ms usually holds good in a service environment too; the manpower, after all remains manpower (or personpower), materials are the inputs necessary for the processes to take place, and the machines are equally translatable as systems and the processes the unit applies to produce the output. Methods, how you actually go about it, equates in manufacturing and service environments, and finally measurement, answers the important need of knowing how we are doing.

Figure 5.2 below outlines a generic approach to the supervisor job and by its definitions provides a perspective for the adaptation of the focus, content, accountability, and the measuring of success of that part of the hierarchy which is crucially important to output.

The supervisor's job in *Kaizen*

Read this in conjunction with Table 3.2 *How the Core Concepts of Kaizen Change Work Processes* in Chapter 3.

Figure 5.1   *A generic approach to the role of supervisor*

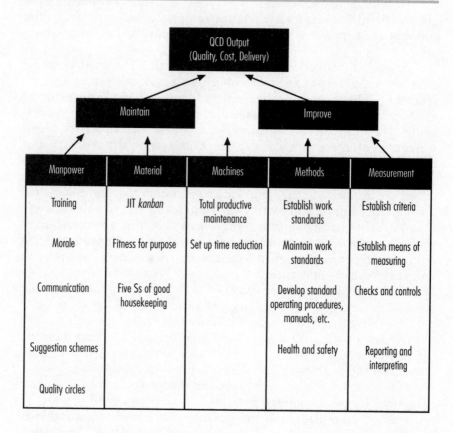

Importantly this kind of approach provides an integrated set of responsibilities and considerable help as to how to structure the job into a number of coherent activities. Formulating and communicating this kind of matrix to employees also provides excellent context and helps the employee understand the nature of the transmission system between the strategic engine and the actual drive wheels.

Gemba, gembutsu and visual supervision

It is a key concept of *Kaizen* that a great deal of the supervisory role is exercised by observation of the work being undertaken at *gemba*. *Gembutsu* is the Japanese term to describe the tangible objects found at *gemba* – the machines, semi-finished and finished products, the physical condition of the environment, etc.

Masaaki Imai[1] tells the story of the new supervisor who was required to stand inside a chalk circle drawn on the floor of the plant for the entire morning to observe what was happening and so gain a clear understanding of the processes involved and how effectively they were working. Boredom set in and finally irritation. In the debriefing which followed however, the new supervisor's lack of understanding of *gemba* and what went on there became obvious. The important lesson was established that without a clear and detailed knowledge of what should happen, and observation of what is actually happening, it becomes impossible to spot deviation or dysfunction in the process. Not being able to do this compromises the supervisor's role to maintain the processes supporting QCD. Further the ability to change and improve the processes virtually vanishes if the base norms of operations are not known.

> *The ability to change and improve the processes virtually vanishes if the base norms of operations are not known.*

> *Comparing the* Kaizen *model with traditional hierarchies it becomes perfectly clear that this sort of approach provides a means of delayering the organization and, by adjusting the focus and content and objectives of the supervisor role, it effects substantial change in a way which is not simply rearranging the deck chairs, but adding relevance and depth to the jobs of supervisor and the rest of the work group. At the same time the organization's enduring strategic needs (QCD) are integrated into the work culture.*

Case Study

Delta Lloyd, an insurance provider in Amsterdam, employs over 2000 people and generates a premium turnover in excess of $2 billion p.a. Typically it was taking two weeks to process paperwork. Investigation showed that each case required an average of only two hours investigation and the rest of the time the paperwork was queuing on people's desks. In other words, a substantial bureaucratic hierarchy was seriously delaying processing, adding to cost, and reducing competitiveness.

To address the problem the company decided to organize itself into a number of teams from 4 to 15 members. Teams were given clearly defined aspects of activity such as issuing policies, adjusting claims or making payments. Clearly defined targets were also set for each team; these embraced revenue and profit, operating targets, customer satisfaction targets and speed of service.

In order to appoint a team leader for each team the company required its 268 managers to reapply for team leader jobs – 58 per cent were successful! As the change was implemented many former line managers found it extremely difficult to operate in the revised parameters of operations. Conversely, some employees appointed to team leader roles found the transition easier.

The net effect on Delta Lloyd is that now typically 70–80 per cent of cases are completed on the same day that they are received.

In analyzing the reasons for this success Delta Lloyd[2] cites first the process of getting the right team leaders as having contributed, and second the radical training programme which accompanied the change.

In the terms we have described above, the success lies as much in changing the focus, the content and the objectives of the team leaders' roles.

KEY POINTS

- The purpose of hierarchies is to locate decision making, accountability and the supervision of work within an authority structure.
- The 'model' of the organization is changing from top down, centrally controlled by rigid procedures to a flatter, delayered structure, with devolved decision making and values and strategy driven.
- Changes to the hierarchy must be accompanied by changes of work focus, work content, accountability, authority and objectives.
- Using the hierarchy as one of the 'change levers' usually requires a lot of unlearning and relearning – especially for line managers.
- *Kaizen* is especially effective in supervisor/worker levels of the organizational structure.
- *Kaizen* offers an excellent generic supervisor job model which fits most organizational strategies, whether manufacturing or service.

Notes

1. Imai, M. (1997) *Gemba Kaizen*, McGraw-Hill.
2. Harrison (1995) 'Organisational Trailblazers' , *Canadian Business Review*.

CHAPTER 6

Change and People

When asked what he had learned after many years of working in the area of quality W. Edwards Deming, the father of the quality control movement, is reputed to have replied 'People are important'.

INTRODUCTION

In the last three chapters we have explored the use of internal processes, the architecture of the organization and its control systems to effect change but the last and most important of the change levers is, of course, the people. Ultimately no change is possible unless the people in the organization enact, support and sustain it.

Arguably one of the most common reasons for the failure of change initiatives is the assumption that people will take a rational and logical approach to the reasons presented for the change and immediately adapt their behaviour to accommodate it. The truth is quite emphatically otherwise. The natural and most comfortable condition of human beings is stability and continuity, people will cleave, often in the face of overwhelming evidence to the contrary, to the tried and trusted. It takes energy to unlearn and relearn, risk is involved, the future is unknown, and if it is going to be different, perhaps it is also threatening. You may argue that this conservatism is not characteristic of all people, and you would be right. In most organizational environments however, risk is rarely rewarded and a great deal of time and energy is spent in eliminating the risky and enshrining as standard operating practice that which has proven to be effective. Once it is well cemented in, predictably it is hard to change.

INDIVIDUAL ACCEPTANCE OF CHANGE

An increasing body of research into successful change implementation supports the view that the psychodynamics of individual change parallels quite closely what happens in an organization which is undergoing change. Both the individual and the organization appear to go through similar discernible stages prior to enacting change. If managers seeking to introduce change into the organization have a clear understanding of these stages they have a useful basis on which to plan the introduction of change into the organization.

Stage 1: negative reactions

The usual tendency is to resist change and it takes a while before the individual can overcome the inertia and start to develop the impetus to change. During this time there is usually ample evidence that things are changing around the individual, but he or she is not yet ready to acknowledge the need to adapt to them. This is an uncomfortable period when people feel negative; they have a sense of anxiety, the cause of which is often hard to define or locate. It is a period when people feel frustrated, angry, defensive and even outraged.

Gradually, as the sense of discontentment and negativity persists, people realize that what they are experiencing is not just a periodic event but is becoming an established pattern. Usually the person is now able to locate the cause of the negative emotion and, as time goes on, he or she is usually able to assign evidence, and to assemble more information and example around the cause. There develops an increasing awareness that 'business as usual' will not eliminate the cause; that current behaviour will not solve the problem, and, at some level, there is awareness that change will be necessary. Sometimes this comes as a sudden breakthrough, often it is simply an increasing accumulation of evidence that forces the realization.

So great is the tendency to stasis, however, that the realization that change is inevitable does not usually trigger the behaviour modification necessary to deal with it. For some the realization itself has an immobilizing effect; people are simply unable to enact a change, trapped like a rabbit in the headlights of an oncoming car. For others there is a certain reward in gaining sympathy and attention as a result of not moving. For most, however, the realization sets in motion serious consideration of alternatives to the current situation. The mechanism seems to be that people start to believe that the consequences of not changing will be more punishing than the difficulty and inconvenience of doing something different, new and untried.

Stage 2: the defining event

For many it is an event which triggers the preparedness to consider change. Sometimes the event is the proverbial 'wake-up call', a shock which provides a new context. Often the event is unrelated to the environment in which the change will be enacted. Sometimes the event is not even recognized except retrospectively when people think about the process that has led to their change. Whatever the nature of the event, the mechanism is that the person gains an insight that somehow enables the reinterpretation of events and provides the resolve, the strength, the trigger to change. The emotional energy which has been consumed in the stage of negative feelings starts to be re-channelled into dealing with the present and the future.

I have heard this situation referred to sometimes as 'being between trapezes': the artiste has let go of the trapeze on which he or she was swinging and has yet to grasp the trapeze to which he or she is going.

Because this state which follows the defining event is uncomfortable, it is often quite brief.

Stage 3: contracting – making the commitment

To strengthen resolve, people often choose to make some public commitment to change. Doing so adds more horsepower to the engine that will drive the change. Contracting with peers or with a boss signals intent and starts the momentum. It also allows the space necessary to plan how the change will be undertaken, and it legitimizes the search for the help of others. It creates personal accountability, it reinforces intent, and sharpens up determination by allocating more negative consequence to the scale pan of maintaining the status quo. Often it has a realizing and invigorating effect on the person; spirits rise, a feeling of well-being returns and energy flows.

Stage 4: self-discovery

Enacting a change that goes through the stages outlined above is usually an educative experience and adds to self-knowledge and self-awareness. Consequent upon it, the person frequently re-appraises a great deal more than the circumstances surrounding the change. New ways of looking at things start to be considered, values are sometimes re-examined, and, often, relationships re-thought.

Stage 5: internalization of change

At this stage the new realities of the changed situation become the norm. The principles and practices which support it are the 'right' ones; a new set of 'the tried and tested' is defined.

ACCEPTANCE OF CHANGE – THE ORGANIZATIONAL PARALLEL

If these five stages are a necessary precondition for the individual to accept the need for and enact change, the question is how organizations behave when confronted by the same need. Because organizations are social systems, composed of people, the parallels are, unsurprisingly, very similar. The table opposite helps explain. In it we show the stage we identified above for individual change, the manifestation of that same stage within the organization, and in the final column we offer some advice as to how the change leaders might cope with each stage.

The higher in the organization the change leader is placed, the more effective that person will be in changing the organization.

It is worth stating that the higher in the organization the change leader is placed, the more effective that person will be in changing the organization.

Table 6.1 *Organizational change model*

Stage	Manifestation in the Organization	Change Leader Role
Negative reactions	Results in the organization show financial downturn, cost increase, market share loss, etc.	Spend time in root cause analysis and develop strategy to reverse the downturn.
	Organization does the same things but harder and more of them.	Start to articulate causes of downturn and the changes necessary to reverse it.
	Morale declines, people get puzzled and frustrated at lack of success.	Enlist as many change agents as possible; gain their commitment to and support for change.
	Blame and recrimination starts.	
	Turf wars start and people start to defend and justify their operations.	Give the change agents the role of disciples – send them out to spread the word.
	Factions develop.	Create a sense of the urgency – the need to change soon.
	Some people leave.	
	People feel threat of job insecurity.	Articulate clearly, unambiguously and precisely what the changes are, and why. Broadcast these continuously, unceasingly, consistently and in as unthreatening a way as possible.
	Perception of the changes which are necessary starts to dawn, bringing: • fears of personal competence and skills to handle new ways • fears of loss of status or authority • accusations of 'flavour of the day' – 'it'll never fly', etc.	Make your message hopeful, upbeat and positive. Keep telling the truth.

Stage	Manifestation in the Organization	Change Leader Role
		Do not 'rubbish' past practices; make it clear they have served well but that events have changed the game.
		Confront the anxieties in the organization and offer reassurance help and support.
		Access and deploy resources to retrain and develop people, provide bridging help, consultancy, etc.
		Reward, celebrate and publicize the slightest movement in support of the change – broadcast success stories.
Defining event	There might be several ways that defining events occur . . . :	Create a defining event(s) away-days, teach-ins, workshops.
	The organization might create a defining event – see next column.	Focus on the fact that your own day-by-day behaviour and that of your 'disciples' is likely to provide defining events for people.
	A particularly serious set of operating results might underscore the necessity for change.	Mould the culture around the new criteria; continuously articulate the new criteria, demonstrate them by your actions and ensure
	Layoffs, closing facilities, divestitures, etc. could highlight the seriousness of the need.	

that the most senior members of the organization also do so consistently. These might provide the defining events people are searching for.

Develop a communications strategy that continuously provides the raw material for defining events by what it reports and the spin with which it reports them.

Demonstrations of involvement often might provide the event for people; cross-functional strategy building sessions, open forums, focus groups for example.

It becomes an essential requirement of the change leader role that the criteria by which the success of the change will be recognized are clearly defined

It is also important that these criteria are cascaded through the organization in so that they affect the way goals and objectives are set at various operating levels.

Rewards, bonuses, promotions, etc. can convince the staff of the organization's intent.

Dismissals, disciplinary proceedings, demotions, etc., i.e. the reverse of the above, might define.

Major internal changes such as:
● process re-engineering
● structural change
● hierarchy changes
can usually underscore intention and hence provide the event.

The example of a colleague or group of colleagues might provide the event.

In the end there must be a defining event for each individual – although the same one might serve a number of people.

Contracting – making the commitment

For most organizations making the commitment will flow from the objective setting procedures the organization employs.

For some, informal agreements might exist between colleagues or groups of colleagues placed, as a result of the change, in different relationships to each other than had previously been the case.

Stage	Manifestation in the Organization	Change Leader Role
	Setting up a new operating team (as might occur in structural changes) requires the tasking of those teams, a redefinition of success criteria and the processes the team will use to achieve them.	While some overarching criteria will probably remain unaltered (financial in particular) the organization will also need feedback loops which inform it as to how it is doing at delivering the change that has been required of it.
	Some organizations have handled it very differently. A chief executive required all his senior vice presidents to write letters of resignation from the 'old' organization and reapply in writing for a position in the new organization. This dramatically underscored the extent of the change involved and the difference in behaviour that would be expected in the new environment.	
Self-discovery	Most organizations will find, if the change introduced has been far-reaching and radical, that they need different skill sets to operate it effectively.	Change leaders need to define the core competencies that the organization will need in the medium and long term to support the strategy that has caused the change. Resources must be made available to develop these core competencies.
	Employees will be seeking training and development opportunities consistent with their new responsibilities.	
	In a more detailed day-to-day operational sense employees will need coaching, counselling and support as they develop and refine their roles.	Having devoted time, high profile and energy to generating the momentum for change, the leader's role will rarely revert to a conventional management one. The same degree of prominence, involvement, sharing of information, and mutual consultation will be expected, and, if employees are not to become cynical, it should be provided.
	Modern change interventions help relate operations in the organization more closely to the strategy. Longer term, as confidence in the new roles grows, employees often seek a greater involvement in strategy and planning as a result.	

PREREQUISITES FOR SUCCESSFUL PERFORMANCE

If the route to change is sometimes tortuous and difficult as we have outlined it above, it is well to think for a moment about the basic prerequisites for individuals to perform adequately in their jobs. What are the conditions which enable employees to operate in any environment whether relatively stable or changing constantly?

At the risk of over simplification, there are few basic conditions which go a long way towards orientating employees, and providing them with the context and parameters in which to function:

- a clear understanding of **purpose** – why we do what we do, not what (see below), but **why**
- an agreed set of **objective**s – what it is you (Boss) expect of me and how we are going to judge whether I have delivered these expectations
- **competence in a series of processes** – the ability to do the job; to operate the equipment, to conduct myself appropriately, to do what needs to be done
- a level of **recognition and support** – somebody giving me feedback as to how I am doing, helping me out when I get in trouble.
- a belief that those around me, especially my boss, have a sense of **confidence** in me and **trust** me to get on with what I need to do without intervention or spying.

Good leaders work to establish and maintain this kind of framework for employees and even when the organization or the unit is engaged in change initiatives, this basic set of principles constitutes the 'contract' between us. Change often implies that the contract is being unilaterally altered and it is establishing a new or different contract that lies at the heart of the change process. Modern employees expect such contracts to be negotiated, not imposed. The extent to which this negotiation is successfully conducted and concluded really defines the effectiveness with which the change is implemented.

> *The leader is attempting to enlist the discretionary effort of the employee to operate in a different way. It is always well to remember that logic alone will certainly not unlock that discretionary effort; it is even more important to remember that without gaining access to it, the change initiative is in danger of running into the sand.*

We are all now trying to build organizations which treat change as part of the base contract, and in this *Kaizen* has something to offer because of its focus on the continuous improvement of processes, quality and customer satisfaction. Incremental improvement in these areas is an aspect of change invariably of strategic importance to the organization and *Kaizen* certainly cements it into the contract in a durable way as we will see later in this chapter. The speed of change though means that organizations also need to be able to enact radical, far-reaching and more fundamental change faster. Few are good at it.

CHANGE AND ORGANIZATIONAL CULTURE

The culture of the organization is the beliefs held by employees of what the prevailing values are within it. The perceptions of the culture revolve around those things that the organization is seen to reward, those on which it is seen to frown and those that it tolerates. Rarely is organizational culture consistent with the official pronouncements of the organization; it is a product of observed behaviour. To the extent that the behaviour of the organization is consistent with its pronouncements, the two are more closely aligned. To the extent they differ, the gap between them is usually bridged by the cynicism of the employees, itself a fairly corrosive cultural trait.

The culture of the organization is the beliefs held by employees of what the prevailing values are within it. The perceptions of the culture revolve around those things that the organization is seen to reward, those on which it is seen to frown and those that it tolerates.

It is true to say, however, that in some organizations there is a culture that is more receptive to change, a culture that is less anxious about the unknown. Such organizations usually have a history of fairly successful and frequent change. Being able to do it, having demonstrated that it can be done, breeds an organizational confidence which more rapidly embraces change and hence accelerates its implementation. Needless to say this is an exceptionally valuable organizational advantage to have developed, one that usually makes the organization more competitive and demonstrates itself in the bottom line.

It takes ages to change the culture of an organization because what people believe about it is what they have observed over extended periods of time. The impetus of even a well designed and orchestrated change initiative is a great deal less powerful than the vested inertia of years of observed events.

John Kotter, one of the change gurus, takes the view that successful change is not a matter of management, it is a matter of leadership. His definitive book on the subject is called *Leading Change*[1] and suggests among its earliest recommendations that those responsible for change develop a sense of urgency. Generating the momentum necessary to displace or start to move the culture is a battle for employee mind share. Even having won the mind share, however, as we have seen above, the change will not start until the defining events finally dislodge employee stasis.

WHAT *KAIZEN* HAS TO OFFER

We have already mentioned that *Kaizen* enshrines the idea of incremental improvement in the 'contract' and hence in the culture as well. By defining incremental improvement not as an objective, but as an operating practice, people in the organization not only find it relatively easier to change, but they come to work in the expectation that it will be happening, that they are responsible for generating it, that they are responsible for implementing it. *Kaizen* creates a change continuum rather than a series of stepped initiatives interspersed with plateaux of 'stability'.

Kaizen achieves this in a number of ways but it is essentially by taking the focus off 'change' and training it instead on process improvement that it achieves most. Process improvement is not about change, it is about making things easier, making things better, making things cheaper. Change is not an initiating factor here, it is a consequence of doing your job properly. That, as a cultural belief, is extremely valuable!

Inculcating and supporting this different form of contract, this cultural belief is not, of course, simply a matter of declaring it to employees. *Kaizen* uses a number of systems and practices to enable employee participation. To demystify and make these concepts easily understood it unsurprisingly has sets of mnemonics to help. These systems and procedures are:

- the PDCA cycle and the SDCA cycle
- the use of standards
- the morning market or morning meeting
- suggestion systems
- small group activities like quality circles.

The PDCA plan-do-check-act cycle

One of the very simplest tools, PDCA drives much of the process of *Kaizen*. One must start with a **plan**, sometimes expressed simply as a target to achieve. Having got the plan, you must **do** it. To test that what you are doing is on track to achieve the plan you must **check**. Finally to ensure that you maintain the improvement you planned for, you must **act** to standardize and ensure what you have done is replicable and consistently repeated.

This is the cycle of continuous improvement repeated and repeated so as to achieve at least incremental improvements, sometimes break-throughs. Plan-do-check-act becomes the organizing principle for the business and all the people in it. Problems are solved by it, objectives achieved by it, and the interests of the organization are advanced by the consistency with which its people follow the cycle.

The SDCA standardize-do-check-act cycle

If PDCA produces the continuous improvement, then SDCA main-tains the base of replicable activities on which improvements rest. Following PDCA we need to **standardize** the improvement produced by our plan. We need to **do,** i.e. repeat the process to the new standard. We need to **check** that the process is in fact achieving the new standard and we need to **act**, either to maintain the process or carry out the cor-rection to achieve the new standard consistently.

Underpinning the PDCA and SDCA cycles is the view that they are ongoing, they represent the underlying how-to of continual improvement whether that is in the quality of the outputs, the ease with which the process is completed, the cost of the process, and the degree of customer satisfaction the output is generating. (The 'cus-tomer', it goes without saying, also means the internal customer; the next step in the process.)

The use of standards

Quality and improvement is only capable of being sustained by con-tinuous replicability of the process by which it is being achieved. Any new process within an organization, whether manufacturing or servic-ing, will potentially have some bugs in it. Using the SDCA cycle to assure that the instabilities, dysfunction or unanticipated problems of the new process are identified and eliminated enables us to create a new standard which we know works.

The standard is the current best way of doing the job so that not only is it the basis of the process but also the base on which improvement must now be built. Standards represent the marker points in the continuum of improvement and at any time, all the members of the work unit must, of course, be working to the current standard.

Each member of a good *Kaizen* team will be able to articulate the standard, and the manager or supervisor, at *gemba* (the place where the process is taking place) will be able to see that the standard is consistently being applied.

The morning market or morning meeting

We read much of creating learning organizations, of providing the environment where employees have the opportunity to develop themselves and at the same time add to the core competencies of the organization. The model of the learning organization has become, for many management gurus, a complex web of interrelated learning networks. *Kaizen*'s approach is simple and fundamental; the best teams meet once per day and sometimes twice, once before the shift, once afterwards, usually for a fairly brief period. The agenda has three components:

- What are we going to do today to meet our QCD output and to improve our base performance?
- What went right/wrong since the last meeting or shift?
- What were the reasons for what went right/wrong?

Sometimes, in a manufacturing environment, yesterday's rejects are there for the team to inspect and to figure out what caused them to be imperfect. It enables the team to identify deviation from the standard, the probable reasons for it, or faults in the standard itself.

Different teams handle it different ways but whatever the agenda, the root intention is to learn from what we have done, to plan together what must be done, and to do so in a manner that is focused on getting better. In Japanese the phrase *jishu kanri* is used for an autonomous team operating in a *Kaizen* manner with a manager or supervisor. Such morning market activities are a precondition for their smooth operation in that the team creates its own goals, evaluates its performance, and has the feedback loops in position to run itself optimally.

Creating an event in the day for employees to come together to plan and to learn has a positive effect on people quite disproportionate to the time it takes. The sense of involvement it generates, the ownership of the standards, the revelations of one's own and the work of others provide an environment which reinforces the core concept of continuous improvement. Involvement generates much higher levels of commitment, greater accountability and ultimately more creative problem solving.

Case Study

Wilson Learning, an international training organization for which I worked at one stage, used to have a daily morning meeting in its Tokyo offices. Wilson used a slogan throughout its operations *'Helping people and organizations become as much as they can be'*. Employees would gather, standing, for no more than 15 or 20 minutes in the reception area of the offices. The managing director, Shozo Mori, would put the question to a few employees on a random basis. What will you do today to help people and organizations become as much as they can be?

Employees would answer briefly but precisely, their replies obviously having been thought through. The staff would then disperse and people would go about their business.

This practice had great value for the staff for it helped to reinforce the purpose of the organization and the relationship of individuals to that purpose on a consistent daily basis. A typical *Kaizen* morning meeting would almost certainly be more targeted in that it would be conducted with an operating team rather than the whole staff. It would also deal much more precisely with the specific operational objectives of the shift or the working day.

Suggestion systems

In the West suggestion systems tend to favour and reward suggestions which save money. In a true *Kaizen* environment, the scope of the suggestion system is far broader and encompasses the core concepts of improvement to processes, quality and customer satisfaction. Ideas to make processes easier, environments less stressful, to make things more interesting and thus minimize the dulling effect of repetitive work are all considered appropriate candidates for suggestions.

A good index of the success of a *Kaizen* system is often taken to be the number and range of suggestions people are generating. Certainly the degree to which the organization has convinced its employees that suggestions are a key to improvement will be reflected in the success of the suggestion system.

It becomes very important that the company responds to all suggestions. This means not only acknowledging them, but undertaking active consideration of their potential. It also means recognizing the good ones and rewarding them. Many *Kaizen* organizations have highly developed employee recognition systems and are imaginative in giving well considered, though not necessarily expensive, rewards for those suggestions which contribute to improvement.

Good organizations also look to the avenue of rejecting suggestions as a means by which the organization can learn and improve. Constructive explanatory activity between managers and *gemba* people nurtures the sense of seriousness with which the organization takes each of its employees and again makes the statement that employees' contributions are key to improvement.

Small group activities

Extending the concept of involving people in improvement is the quality circle. Usually this is a cross-functional team with the task of effecting improvement in an environment broader than the scope of an individual operating team or *jishu kanri*. Serving on such groups is often seen as developmental and an opportunity for members to gain recognition and sometimes reward. In some organizations this kind of activity is undertaken outside normal working hours, which gives an indication of the high perceived value accorded to it by participants.

It is the sense of involvement, of decision making at *gemba*, of the value of the contribution of the individual which not only makes these group activities successful but reinforces the interdependency of the organization and its employees around the concept of continuous improvement.

KEY POINTS

- No change is possible in an organization unless it is supported, implemented and maintained by the people in the organization.
- People do not easily accept change and there are stages we all go through before we are prepared to change what we do.
- Organizations implementing change behave in a way which is very similar to how individuals behave.

- Leading (as distinct from managing) this change process requires an assertive and untiring intervention by the change leaders.

- To do their jobs properly, people need a clear five part 'contract' with their bosses and with the organization – purpose, objectives, competence in processes, recognition and support, confidence and trust.

- Organizational culture, the belief systems which prevail in an organization, often have to change before other forms of change can be successfully implemented. Changing culture is a long process.

- *Kaizen* offers a number of ways of initiating and sustaining continuous improvement, primarily in the 'contract' between employee and the organization.

- *Kaizen* also offers systems and practices which help the employee facilitate change:
  - the PDCA cycle to change things, the SDCA cycle to maintain change
  - the use of standards to benchmark the effect of change and to provide the platform for the next level of improvement
  - the morning market or morning meeting to develop the team's ability to learn from what it does
  - suggestion systems to enlist the force of *gemba* in continuous improvement
  - group activities like quality circles to involve people and tap into their experience.

Note

1.   Kotter, J. (1996) *Leading Change*, Harvard Business School Press.

CHAPTER 7

Designing a Change Programme

Introduction

———

Force Field Analysis

———

Generating an Action Plan and Establishing
Measuring Criteria

———

Using Critical Success Factors

———

The AA Insurance Case Study

———

Key Points

'. . . the victorious army first realizes the conditions for victory, and then seeks to engage in battle. The vanquished army fights first, and then seeks victory.'

SUN TZU, sixth century Chinese general and strategist

INTRODUCTION

The excitement and enthusiasm which is sometimes generated by the organization's strategists as they formulate a way forward often means that careful planning to implement the supporting changes is ignored in the rush for action. Most organizations will find that time taken in planning change is a sensible investment. As with all planning, if it is approached at the strategic level, that is what Sun Tzu (above) describes as the '. . . conditions for victory . . .', rather than the tactics of implementation, a more robust and successful plan emerges.

One of the most useful means of planning is to employ a variant of Kurt Lewin's[1] force field analysis, a methodology for problem analysis and planning. Force field analysis has a number of structured steps which support a graphical convention. It is more important to follow the steps than to become too entrapped in the niceties of the discipline.

FORCE FIELD ANALYSIS

The basic steps in using the technique are to:

- develop a clear definition of where you want to be
- develop a clear definition of where you are
- determine the forces which favour getting where you want to be – the enablers
- determine the forces which resist getting where you want to be – the constrainers
- review and prioritize trying to indicate the relative weight or influence of both the enablers and the constrainers
- generate solutions to maximize the influence, weight or effectiveness of the enablers

- generate solutions to minimize the influence, weight or hindrance exercised by the constrainers
- convert to an action plan
- generate criteria which will enable you to know that you are achieving the change you are planning – milestones, etc.

Graphically the force field diagram looks like this.

Figure 7.1   *Force field graphic*

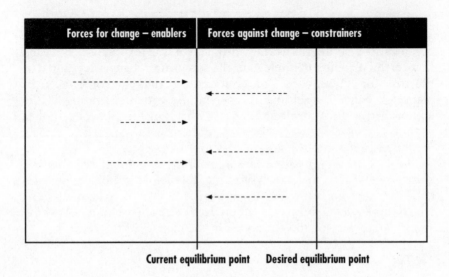

Forces for change – enablers	Forces against change – constrainers	

Current equilibrium point   Desired equilibrium point

The length of the line behind the arrowhead for both enablers and constrainers shows the relative power of each of the items around the current equilibrium point. This is usually a fairly subjective and inexact set of estimates. Enablers and constrainers are rarely of the same nature, so that in the end one is comparing apples and oranges. My experience though is that the debate generated in a group of planners trying to gauge relative importance of each, helps clarify and define the problem and so starts the process of solution.

Underlying the thinking behind force field analysis is that to effect the change the organization needs to 'unfreeze' the current situation and then 're-freeze' it in the desired situation. The forces which are responsible for fixing the current equilibrium point, must be altered so that they fix the desired equilibrium point. The model is highly mechanistic, but it helps to understand the scope of the change.

Defining where you want to be

Almost every successful change initiative is propelled by a powerful and widely shared vision of the end destination. It is the absolute duty of the people initiating the change to be very clear and unambiguous about what the end results look like. Communicating, sharing, describing and enlarging the vision is among the first and most critical generators of the momentum, which will eventually drive the change forward.

If the word 'vision' seems itself imprecise, be under no illusions as to the requirement for hard edged descriptors to help members of the organization to understand. To be effective the vision must be seen to address a strategic need and have high face validity to those who listen to it.

Those working on the change initiative must share the vision and have a deep understanding of it. Without this, it will prove hard to enact the change and the lack of a shared view becomes immediately apparent as you grapple with a first pass at constructing the components of the force field analysis.

Almost every successful change initiative is propelled by a powerful and widely shared vision of the end destination. It is the absolute duty of the people initiating the change to be very clear and unambiguous about what the end results look like.

An effective way of defining the vision is to use the four major change levers described in Chapters 3–6 of this book. That is being able to articulate:

- *how the **work processes** will differ*
- *how the **organizational structure** will differ*
- *how the **hierarchy** will differ*
- *how **people's behaviour** will differ.*

Defining where we are now

This is not usually an area of great debate when force field analyses are in use. Where we are now is usually described only in terms of how it differs from where we want to be. Sometimes where we are now might be at a milestone along a road towards where we want to be, and this should be acknowledged.

Defining enablers and constrainers; reviewing and prioritizing them

Again, in my experience this is a salutary team exercise. The best results happen when the change team jointly compile these two critical lists and explore their definitions. This is also a time for truth telling. Change initiatives often run into the ground because of a reluctance to share the extent of the change envisaged and somehow to pretend that what we have in mind is not really that different. It becomes important, in identifying what must be covered by the change programme, to be realistic and honest.

Remember that people support changes where the benefits are seen to be personal to them, immediate in their impact, and certain in delivering expectations.

Part of the problem is that the enablers often tend to provide a future pay-off while the constrainers are here and now. The enablers are also often speculative, the constrainers are real and certain. The enablers will benefit the organization, the constrainers will affect the people.

In terms of planning to strengthen the enablers and minimize the effect of the constrainers, remember that people support changes where the benefits are seen to be personal to them, immediate in their impact, and certain in delivering expectations. People do not support things where the benefits are seen to be corporate, where the benefit is delayed or when it is not certain that a benefit will in fact accrue.

Some Typical Enablers	Some Typical Constrainers
The change supports the competitive strategy.	People are cynical about yet another change.
The MD supports it.	It's not clear whether the whole Board supports it.
'X' operating department will have their problems solved by it.	'Y' and 'Z' operating departments will have their activities curtailed by it.
The job(s) will be easier to do; productivity will improve.	It will require immediate capital investment.
There will be re-training opportunities.	There will be redundancies.
We have the IT base to support it.	We lack the skill base for implementation.

Generating solutions to maximize the effect of the enablers and minimize the effect of the constrainers

All changes stand or fall, as we have already said, on the preparedness of the people whom they affect to embrace them; if this is to happen be guided by this lore . . .

> *To the extent that both the rewards for compliance with the change and the 'punishments' for non-compliance are made personal, immediate, and certain, then the people will support the change.*

Brainstorming techniques often help generate a number of ways of handling both the enablers and the constrainers. The change team will enjoy this activity and, by generating a large number of alternatives, however off-the-wall they might be, a wider potential range of ideas from which courses of action can be chosen will improve the creativity of the plan.

Parallel to brainstorming the change team also needs the discipline of understanding how to use the four change levers. Ask the question of each of the enablers or constrainers:

- how might we use **work process** to minimize/maximize the effect of the constrainers/enablers?
- how might we use **structure** to minimize/maximize the effect of the constrainers/enablers?
- how might we change the **hierarchy** to minimize/maximize the effect of the constrainers/enablers?
- how might we affect **people** to minimize/maximize the effect of the constrainers/enablers?

Consult the summary of key points at the end of Chapter 2, and look at the individual key points summaries for Chapters 3–6 to refresh your understanding of each of the change levers, then assess your scope for dealing with the elements of the force field.

GENERATING AN ACTION PLAN AND ESTABLISHING MEASURING CRITERIA

It is a relatively easy step from the Generating Solutions exercise above to action planning. Organizations use a wide range of planning systems so just use the one that best fits or with which you are most familiar. Be sure that it specifies:

- what must be done
- all the things that must be done
- by whom
- by when.

You must also be clear about how you will know that something has been achieved. An action of itself is simply a precursor to achieving a result. The result must be defined and have some measurable characteristics.

You must also be clear about how you will know that something has been achieved. An action of itself is simply a precursor to achieving a result. The result must be defined and have some measurable characteristics. Spending time in defining the metrics by which the team will know that an action has achieved the desired result is, again, a sound investment in time. Reaching agreement about the measurable result often re-defines the action itself. Sometimes it further develops the plan by shedding more light on people's perspectives of need. At least it will help clarify and refine the plan.

A further discipline of planning is actually to transfer the plan into some form of critical path analysis. Programme evaluation and review techniques (PERT) really help and there is also lots of good planning software about. Again, using one of these formal project management systems will further refine and clarify your plan and hence improve the chances of its success.

The memorable quotation about 'plans being useless but planning being indispensable' is ascribed to General Eisenhower. If you do not already know this, or your team insufficiently appreciates it, handling a major change will convince you. My advice is to set out to prove Eisenhower right rather than to ruefully discover, after the event, that he probably was.

USING CRITICAL SUCCESS FACTORS

A critical success factor is something that simply must go right in order to achieve your goals. Independently of the planning exercise, I advise before rather than after, try to establish the critical success factors for your change.

A way of doing this is to take the where-we-want-to-be description and re-phrase it in the past tense. This enables you to look at the description as if it has already been successfully accomplished.

Spend a little time getting you and your team into a future perspective, looking back at a successful achievement. Then ask yourself these questions.

- What were the three most important things that we did to manage this change so successfully?
- What three things would my boss say we did to manage this change so successfully?
- What three things would the people most affected by the change say that we did to manage the change most effectively?
- What three things would our competitors say we did to manage this change so successfully?

Obviously the same thing may come up under more than one heading. Sometimes the same core thing surfaces under slightly different guises or perhaps viewed from a slightly different perspective.

Take feedback from the team and jointly develop a list of the critical success factors. Typically there are ten or less, of which three or four distinguish themselves as being overwhelmingly important. The fact is that in time, all of them will prove to be important, but different priorities will emerge as the plan goes forward.

Typical critical success factors might be as follows.

- We solicited the support of the entire Board in communicating the changes.
- The training programme we used was really effective.
- A new reward system helped people adapt to changed processes.
- Redundancy issues were handled fairly and humanely, and were seen to be.

Note that they are written in the past tense. Note that they usually define an outcome rather than a how-to (the how-to is for action planning). Note that they are apples and oranges as well and sometimes difficult to prioritize.

The AA Insurance Case Study

An exceptionally well reported case study[2] chronicles the extensive changes that have been enacted at AA Insurance Services between 1995 and 1998. That part most relevant to the design of a change programme is summarized below but the whole case repays close study.

AAIS, in common with all other insurance organizations was deeply affected by Direct Line which redefined the traditional broker based insurance business. AAIS found that their revenues were falling and that in two years they suffered an 80 per cent erosion in profits.

Initially AAIS undertook massive cost cutting, closing one of their three operating centres and enacting extensive redundancies through the other two. The workforce was dramatically reduced from 3000 to below 2000 and management spans of control were also increased.

Having staunched the losses AAIS then set about creating a new vision to carry the company forward. An opinion survey conducted among staff showed that the staff had an unfavourable view, even by the standards of companies undergoing change, of a number of areas such as their sense of strategic direction, the training they were receiving, the degree to which they felt empowered, etc. In retrospect the company identifies a 'survivors' syndrome' felt among those members of staff who were not made redundant. This was characterized by a lack of trust in the management and low motivation.

AAIS launched the Osprey programme, which sought to further reduce costs, to improve customer service, to develop IT capability and to increase productivity. Essentially this programme was a business process re-engineering approach. A number of characteristics mark it out as distinctively different though. First it was conducted internally by AAIS people themselves. Second it drew heavily on the input of front line staff; third it was characterized by a high level of communication throughout the organization.

In the event, Osprey was originally seen by staff as a further means to achieve redundancy. Communication, involvement, an immediate degree of success, and the extensive retraining of people eventually caused the programme to be accepted as the channel through which staff could contribute. In the event the programme achieved dramatic productivity increases.

AAIS also introduced the Investors in People (IiP)programme which, too, was greeted with cynicism. The management found that to clothe IiP in altruism was counterproductive and the programme needed to show the relationship between people development and the success of the business. What emerged was a model showing happy people creating happy customers and hence happy numbers.

The company is now working to consolidate its enviable brand, to improve its operational excellence and, with greater difficulty apparently, to develop continuous imaginative improvement.

In summarizing what AAIS has learned, they cite the involvement of individuals in the change process is essential. They also feel they underestimated the degree to which the 'survivor syndrome' would be a constrainer to change. They warn that it is impossible to overestimate the investment in time spent in consultation and energy spent in communication. They found that the trust of the workforce was regained only slowly as management was seen to do what they said they would.

Sometimes people use the critical success factors as the front end of the action planning and that is a reasonable approach. The only caution to offer is that while critical success factors are, by definition, the most important things to get right, they do not cover the entire spectrum of everything that may have to be done to enact the change. Identifying and working at these things remains at the heart of the planning process.

We do not know whether the use of a force field analysis approach would have revealed the richness of experience that AAIS has gained as a result of the transformation of the company. By all accounts though the planning and introduction of Osprey and of IiP demonstrates the depth of planning and the consistency of application that characterizes successful change initiatives.

KEY POINTS

- Major changes must be designed and planned in detail to be successful.
- Force field analysis is one of the models which can be used.
- Essentially the forces which constrain the change must be minimized and the forces that enable or assist change must be maximized.
- Change planning relies on a really clear and shared view of where we want to be in the future – the vision.
- The four major levers of change: processes, structure, hierarchy and people should be deployed to help identify ways of dealing with enablers and constrainers.
- Detailed action planning which includes defined and measurable objectives is essential.
- Project management techniques or software also helps.
- Use critical success factors – the things that have to go right in order to succeed – as a precursor to planning.

Notes

1. Kurt Lewin, 1890–1947, was a German-born psychologist, who studied human motivation and group dynamics. He worked mostly in the USA and was one of the earliest social psychologists.

2. Smith, B. and Hall, S. (1998) 'Taking AA Insurance from Recovery to Sustainable Growth', *Long Range Planning*, 31 (4).

CHAPTER 8

Kaizen *Processes to Initiate Change*

Introduction

———

The PDCA Process

———

Considering the Next Steps

———

Some Case Experience

———

Case Study

———

Two-day *Kaizen*

———

Key Points

*'. . . the ingenious are always fanciful, and the **truly** imaginative never otherwise than analytic.'*

EDGAR ALLAN POE (1809–45), US poet.

INTRODUCTION

Kaizen provides a process, a format for enacting change that is sometimes called the *Kaizen* story. Essentially it is a series of sequential steps that can be used to guide a group, often an improvement team, through the process of identifying and fixing a problem. The *Kaizen* story does not depend on there being a *Kaizen* working culture within the organization, it can as readily be used by any team seeking a disciplined and analytical approach to problem solving. Building on the words of Edgar Allan Poe above, it is often the discipline and analysis that produces the truly imaginative solution, rather than fanciful ingenuity.

THE PDCA PROCESS

As you follow through the steps of the *Kaizen* story, remember the PDCA mnemonic – **P**lan, **D**o, **C**heck, **A**ct which we discussed in Chapter 6; it provides one of the underlying disciplines on which the *Kaizen* story is built.

The process follows these steps.

- Identifying the problem.
- Understanding the current status, the base from which you are trying to improve.
- Finding the root cause of the problem.
- Planning what you will do to fix it.
- Implementing the plan.
- Confirming the effect of the implementation.
- Establishing a new standard to consolidate the change.
- Considering the next steps.

Let us look at each of the steps in the process.

Identifying the problem (part of the **Planning** element of PDCA)

Problems are usually of two kinds. The first is a deviation from an established norm, i.e. something is going wrong. A rise in error rate, a decline in market share might be examples of these kinds of problem. The second kind of problem arises when we do not know how to achieve an outcome. We might need to improve our customer satisfaction for example, or we might want to enter a new market. Here the problem is not simply restoring a situation to equilibrium, it requires the need to achieve something new or different. Shifts of strategy may require this, or the organization might be making a tactical change to respond to the operating environment.

For the line manager the problem usually presents itself in an operational guise and it usually becomes necessary to determine what actually underlies the manifestation of the problem. To determine this there are two routes to pursue; first we must be certain that we understand the core of the problem and that we are not simply trying to relieve a symptom. Second we need to expand our understanding of it.

Understanding the current status (also part of the **Planning** element of PDCA)

Before we do anything we need to assemble as much information about the current situation as we can. Two courses of action are advised.

Unsurprisingly, *Kaizen*'s first piece of advice is to go to *gemba*, the place where the problem has revealed itself, the proverbial coalface, where the supporting processes take place. Look carefully at what is happening there, look at the *gembutsu*, those things which are physically there; the output of the processes, the machines which are in use, the environment of the work unit, etc.

Kaizen also advises that if immediate corrective or palliative action can be taken, it should be, then and there. While this is pretty obvious, part of the thinking behind it is to create a degree of urgency among the operators to understand the problem and to contribute to its solution.

Kaizen, in search of root cause analysis always advises that you ask 'why' four times:

Q: *Why are you checking both the computer record and a manual record?*

A: Because the computer record is sometimes not up to date.

Q: *Why is it not up to date?*
A: Because there is a bottleneck in the data input section so they do a manual record from the incoming mail every day as well.

Q: *Why is there a bottleneck in the data input section?*
A: Because the new software is very complicated and nobody understands it yet.

Q: *Why don't people understand it?*
A: Because they're still debugging it and nobody's been trained on it yet.

From the above we can see that a problem which may have manifested itself as a delay in response time to telephone enquirers has actually moved to a software debugging and training issue in an upstream set of work processes.

Besides the why-four-times the other course of action in trying to understand the current situation is to start to collect data on it. Again at *gemba* we can start to institute information gathering, thus again serving the agenda of involving the people in the problem and its solution, but we can gather data from other sources as well.

Finding the root cause (still part of the **Planning** element of PDCA)

Root cause analysis is a central tenet of *Kaizen*. It implies firstly that we are solving the right problem, not merely an operational manifestation of it. Secondly it implies that we get to the root of what is actually causing the problem. If we have to fix it, be certain that we are fixing the right thing!

Root cause analysis uses any of a number of the classic problem-solving tools. As with any set of analytical tools the quality of the data is crucial. Selecting a way of evaluating the data so that they become information, and accurate information, might, for example, start with tally charts which record the incidence of events which are material to the problem. You might then move onto pareto analysis, fishbone analysis, histograms and scatterplots to determine incidence, source, relative importance, etc. The classic Ishikawa Seven[1] will usually provide all the appropriate tools for the evaluation of data needed for most root cause analysis. Competence in this relatively simple set of tools is necessary at all levels in the organization. Happily many of them (e.g. graphs, histograms, etc.) are now built into most standard office computer software, providing easy access and speedy analysis.

While good analytical data are required for all problem solving, the intuition of supervisors, the experience of the people at gemba *and precedent within the organization will all help to contribute to the identification of root causes.*

While good analytical data are required for all problem solving, the intuition of supervisors, the experience of the people at *gemba* and precedent within the organization will all help to contribute to the identification of root causes. Ishikawa famously enjoined everybody to mistrust all data. He held that statistics and information were, and are, often assembled to comfort senior management, to confirm beliefs or prejudices rather than to convey reality. This is undoubtedly true, and a healthy disbelief must be balanced with a level of respect for vested knowledge if root cause analysis is to be effective.

Planning what you will do to fix the problem (still part of the **Planning** element of PDCA)

Beyond the obvious advice of involving people at *gemba* in planning and implementation, *Kaizen* offers no special insights into the planning process. Fishbone analysis is very frequently used both in analysis and in planning, and, because it presents good visual condensation of a lot of disparate facts, it has value in communicating the planning process to participants.

Brainstorming approaches are sometimes used, and this helps in that it often generates many more alternatives from which to select to put a plan together.

More importantly, the planning process is seen as part of the PDCA continuum so that it anticipates the need to **C**heck later, after **D**oing. This may sometimes encourage planners to concentrate on what will constitute the criteria for evaluating whether the plan is successful. If you are committed to **C**, the **C**heck, what will you be checking for? How will you know the plan is working?

Implementing the plan (the **Doing** element of PDCA)

In *Kaizen* **D**oing and **C**hecking should really be written as a single word. Again the disciplines imposed by a PDCA approach simply dictate the way people work. This might sometimes involve piecemeal implementation in order that components of a complex plan can be separately evaluated or checked as part of total programme of implementation.

Either way, the involvement of the people at *gemba* is a key commitment.

Confirming the effect of implementation (the **Check** element of PDCA)

Here we return to the **P**lanning phase during which we specified the nature of the measures. Evaluation of the success of what we have changed is reviewed both in its component parts and the degree to which it is affecting the totality of the problem we are trying to solve.

Establishing a new standard (the **Act** element of PDCA)

If it is working, if it has solved the problem, *Kaizen* now moves to establish the new standard. Remember that standard is defined as the 'current right way of doing the job'. Note that in using the word 'current' in an environment of continuous improvement there is an implicit assumption that a better way not only exists, but also will be developed.

The enormous importance of creating the standard cannot be overstated. Standards are, themselves, major elements of operational discipline. They are the basis on which the large international quality measures IS 9000/QS 9000, etc. are established and maintained. They provide a number related advantages as well:

- they prevent the recurrence of error and enable the continuous replication of agreed definitions of outputs
- they help enshrine know-how and expertise, they also facilitate the transference of expertise

- they provide the bases for measuring performance, for auditing how we are doing
- they help the people at *gemba* (or anyone else involved for that matter) to understand the relationships between causes and effects
- they provide the new foundation on which improvement, development, enhancement will be founded – this is key in the *Kaizen* environment of continuous improvement
- they provide the basis for establishing and measuring training needs and the success of training interventions.

In short, standards are inseparable from the concept of maintaining quality and achieving continuous improvement.

CONSIDERING THE NEXT STEPS

This bridges the move from PDCA to **SDCA** – see Chapter 6.

We now have our problem cured, or we are delivering the objective we set ourselves, we also have a new standard – two questions now arise.

Will the new standard continue to deliver the specified outcome? This triggers the SDCA routine where we need systems or processes to assure that it continues to work. The **S** is the standard. We need in our supervision and in our operating self discipline to assure that the standard is consistently being observed that people are **D**oing (the **D** of SDCA) what we established as the best way of doing it.

Standards are inseparable from the concept of maintaining quality and achieving continuous improvement.

We need also to **C**heck (the **C** of SDCA) that it is continuing to deliver the outcome which we have specified. If it is not we need to Act (the **A** of SDCA) and the way we act is to re-embark on the whole *Kaizen* process outlined above, to start the *Kaizen* story again.

If it is working we focus on the next question *How do we improve on the quality, process or customer satisfaction of the work unit's outputs?* In other words, we invoke the continuous improvement type of thinking which, by and large, covers the second type of problem we outlined above; the kind of problem where we need to achieve something different from what we are doing.

Deploying the *Kaizen* process to initiate change by embarking on the *Kaizen* story then produces incremental improvement and hence continuing ongoing change. This can be expressed graphically as in Fig. 8.1 below.

Figure 8.1   *How PDCA and SDCA produce ongoing change*

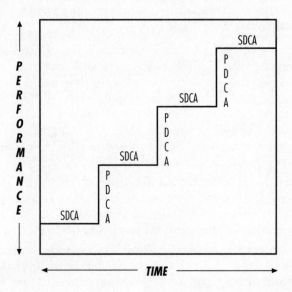

Much in Kaizen *depends on common sense becoming enshrined in day-to-day practice, in the way people approach things. The* Kaizen *story is simply a process for the rigorous application of common sense. When common sense itself becomes the standard, a* Kaizen *culture starts to emerge and it usually seems comfortable to those who use it.*

Some Case Experience

Western organizations sometimes have problems in enacting the behavioural changes which are needed to move towards an environment of continuous improvement. Researchers at Bowling Green University[2] tracked seven organizations as they went through the process of developing their quality improvement programmes. Two persistent difficulties were identified.

- Initial gains made in improvement were not consolidated by incremental reinforcers following them and thus making them common practice. Examples cited were that while the initial clean-up of the working environment successfully produced improvement, the condition of the workplace was allowed to deteriorate again with consequent drop off in performance. In *Kaizen* terms this would be diagnosed as PDCA working OK but not being supported by SDCA.

  In *Kaizen* this is referred to as the 'sawtooth effect'; the graph of improvement does not move on a steady upward trajectory as in Fig. 8.1, but rather shows gains and losses following each other with an overall flat, unimproved level of performance.

- A more intractable problem occurred in the study though, associated with the difficulty team leaders had in balancing production targets and improvement targets. Team leaders found that running them both in tandem proved difficult and either one or the other suffered. Predictably, as in most business environments, it was the improvement criteria which were abandoned when choices had to be made. This is a difficult problem to deal with because its solution lies in an organizational culture that believes in, and is committed to, continuous improvement. If there is no deeply held belief in the strategic advantage that it offers an organization, the idea will always compete unsuccessfully with the imperatives of immediate production targets.

Case Study

Alexander Doll, a New York based company manufacturing a product line of collectible dolls, went into receivership in 1995. The company was bought by TBM Consulting who specialize in *Kaizen* consultancy in partnership with a New York bank, Gefinor USA. This is what happened.[3]

Applying the problem solving principles of *Kaizen*, a cross-functional improvement team went to *gemba* and collected data at all stages of the production process. Among the first problems identified was the company's use of batch processing production systems. This meant that before each of the separate processes literally hundreds of semi-completed dolls were queuing for the next process. Besides inflating the inventory of work in progress, the unfinished dolls sustained damage as batches were moved from process to process.

The improvement team replaced the batch process system with a continuous flow line and consolidated the line into one area whereas individual processes had previously been dispersed throughout the plant. Now dolls moved down a production line which was 40 feet long rather than the 630 feet each doll had travelled previously.

Results were impressive; the production time for an individual doll fell from 90 days to 90 minutes. Unfinished inventory of dolls fell from 29,000 to 34, and the square footage utilized by the process fell from over 2000 square feet to under 1000. Productivity per capita went from 8 dolls per person per day to 25.

The degree of change needed in such a reorganization is of course radical and far-reaching. The CEO of the company cites the use of cross-functional teams drawn from a long serving and dedicated workforce in problem solving and change implementation as one of the two key characteristics of success.

There is an increasing amount of evidence, both practical experience and structured research to suggest that if organizations are to achieve a measure of change through continuous improvement then two characteristics are necessary:

- a structured process such as the *Kaizen* story outlined above
- competence and capability in the tools of problem solving and ultimately TQM tools as well.

TWO-DAY *KAIZEN*

In his definitive book on *gemba Kaizen* Masaaki Imai[4] describes this express system developed by Nissan Motor Company to provide a rapid response mechanism.

The process starts with getting very clear about the target that is being aimed for. This clarity must focus, for example, down to a given production line which must produce a given increase in output by a specified date.

An elite team is put together often consisting of, for example, the plant manager, supervisors and operators. The team does as much pre-work as possible in terms of clarifying and focusing on the problem, acquainting themselves with the line in question, and clearly formulating the desired outcome.

On a given day the team visits the line and explains to the operators the context and purpose of their visit. Team members then observe the line in acute detail and record their observations.

The team then meets and against a specified deadline, usually the late afternoon, they must agree the action they are going to take to meet the target they have set themselves for the line. The discussion may entail members returning to the line to clarify or check.

Once a series of decisions is reached, the team returns to the line to check their recommendations with the operators. In the ensuing discussion a final plan is formed.

Maintenance people who have been on standby against the finalization of the plan are then called in to make the necessary changes to the line. This might imply moving machinery and equipment, moving in new equipment, altering the layout of the line or parts of it, etc.

Once the alterations are completed, typically by about 10.00 p.m., the line is then started and operated by the team to check out any unforeseen problems or difficulties. Only after this has taken place can the team go to bed – sometimes this can take all night.

Next morning the shift starts with an explanation by the team to the operators of what has been done overnight, and how the line will now operate. The line is started again and the team remains with the operators for the first hour or two of operation to ensure that everything is going well. Difficulties and problems are ironed out during this period and adjustments made to complete the process by the middle of the day.

Operations are then monitored and a summary and wrap-up session takes place.

After the closure of the session at the end of the second day, the SDCA processes must of course still take place; new standards being set, checked and the changes consolidated.

This two-day process is really no different in the order and disciplines it follows than is the process of the *Kaizen* story. It differs only in the speed with which the process is undertaken and the degree and intensity of resources that are thrown at the problem.

KEY POINTS

- *Kaizen* offers a simple eight step approach to problem solving and enacting change; this is sometimes called the *Kaizen* story.
- The approach seeks to isolate the root causes of the problem and uses both 'going to *gemba*' as well as data collection and interpretation to get to the bottom of it.
- The process relies heavily on PDCA (Plan, Do, Check and Act) to identify the problem and fix it.
- Setting new standards – the current best way to do the job – provides the line manager with a means of defining the changes.
- Switching to SDCA (Standardize, Do, Check, Act) cements the change into the operating practices.
- Failure to follow the SDCA route produces the sawtooth effect – temporary improvements which are not sustained.
- Continuous improvement programmes often lose the battle if production targets are falling short.

Notes

1. Professor Kauro Ishikawa of Tokyo University was one of the earlier gurus; his seven problem solving tools are well known.

2. Choi, Rungtusanatham and Kim (1997) 'Continuous Improvement on the Shopfloor; Lessons from Small and Midsize Firms', *Business Horizons*, Nov–Dec.

3. Maynard 'A Company is Turned Round through Japanese Principles', *Nations Business*, 84 (2).

4. Imai, M. (1997) *Gemba Kaizen*, McGraw Hill.

CHAPTER 9

The Implications of Quality for
Change in the Organization

'The best is the enemy of the good.'
VOLTAIRE (1694–1778), French philosopher

INTRODUCTION

Most organizations accept that they are committed to continued quality improvement of their goods and services, that they are committed to continued improvement of their processes and systems, and that they are committed to a continual need to enhance their customer satisfaction. These strategic requirements are preconditions for staying in business and competing for an ever more demanding customer.

Strategic focus on quality, however, is an extremely exacting set of disciplines and it demands a progressively increasing commitment from the organization. First of all the quality base is consistently moving upwards. In Voltaire's terms above, what is the best today is likely to be only the good in the very near future. In almost all industries the power of competition is constantly establishing new customer benchmarks and raising customer expectations.

All of this implies that organizations need, to compete, a readiness to embrace the ongoing changes necessary to maintain their strategic market position. This chapter provides a model to help understand the implications of keeping up with the moving target of quality.

QUALITY AS STRATEGY

If we all agree that the minimum standards of quality are perpetually on the move, we must also agree that the scope of what constitutes quality is also enlarging all the time. A useful handle on quality has been provided for us in the work of research organizations[1] which are monitoring quality developments around the world. Here is a useful set of five definers.

- *Conformance* – this means the product or service conforms to specification; early quality work referred to conformance as 'fitness for purpose'.
- *Reliability* – this implies that the product or service performs consistently and does not break down.

- *Performance* – this implies that the product or service has a broader range of capabilities or features which the customer perceives as valuable.

- *Customization* – here we have a quality requirement which enables the organization to adapt the basic product or service to meet the specific and possibly unique demands of the customer.

- *Customer service* – here we need a series of capabilities which imply mastery of customer service. At this level of quality the organization will be able to add value to the relationship between itself and its clients in a number of ways like speed of delivery, availability, after sales support, international provision, etc.

It is plain to see that collectively, these five levels of quality capability which the organization must seek to build eventually constitute the basis of its differentiation from its competitors. They are, in fact, a substantial part of the strategy the organization will follow in providing certain categories of products and services to certain categories of markets.

Recent surveys of organizations' approach to quality indicate that those serving more sophisticated customers are all having to operate at the fourth and fifth levels. Japanese companies in particular tend to be well into the complexities of stages four and five. This is probably about what one would expect. Japanese organizations have had great international success in the past in deploying the quality tool to gain market share, probably most notably in the car wars of the US auto car market. It is unsurprising that they will attempt to play this strategic card again . . . and again . . . and again . . .!

QUALITY AS ORGANIZATIONAL DEVELOPMENT

Obviously organizations should seek to improve their performance across the whole spectrum of quality, but this often proves too difficult to achieve all at the same time. Some of the elements of the 'quality staircase',[2] as it is sometimes called, are obviously interrelated. Reliability, for example, cannot be achieved unless the product or service conforms to specification. Similarly performance cannot be achieved without reliability. The history of Britain's Jaguar in the 1970s is just such a telling example – a car of superb performance in those rare periods when it was not in for repair.

Organizations are better advised to regard the quality staircase as a developmental track that maps out a substantial change programme with a series of sequential steps. The context which this approach provides organizations is a major means of orientating employees to the eventual scope of the change envisaged and its strategic importance.

Organizations are advised to regard the quality staircase as a developmental track that maps out a substantial change programme with a series of sequential steps.

Handling each step in turn also allows the organization to concentrate and focus its resources at given stages. As each stage is achieved, as measured by the criteria the organization has defined, the changes which support it must be consolidated into practice; in *Kaizen* terms a standard is created and the SDCA sequence cements the standard into operations as the current best way of doing the job. Without this consolidation the organization's overall quality improvement will be 'sawtooth' and it may even lose ground in earlier stages.

In the previous chapter we mentioned that there is strong evidence to support the view that lasting change is not achieved unless it is approached with a highly structured process (like the *Kaizen* story). It is also not achieved unless employees are trained in the analytical tools, the Ishikawa Seven, for example, to analyze and fix the problem. When we arrange these competencies along the developmental quality staircase we have a well-mapped route to enact our change initiative, and a means of getting there.

THE SWITCH OF ORGANIZATIONAL FOCUS

As we look at the quality staircase it is possible to see that the organization has to change its focus as it moves through the various stages. At the compliance and the reliability levels, the focus is essentially internal. We are ensuring that the processes and systems we use to make the product or provide the service are meeting the conformance criteria – zero defects, in fact.

Again we are internally focused on our own systems and processes to assure that reliability is achieved. We are working to assure that the product or service works to specification all the time, does not break down, is not in need of constant laborious maintenance or extensive repair.

In both of these initial steps we are at *gemba*, we are dealing with the processes and systems by which the product or service is made or developed. As we move to the performance step, however, the focus shifts from internal systems and processes, and fixes intently on the customer. If performance is what is required, how might we define that performance? The answer, of course is that we must use the customers' yardsticks for performance. Further, since customers frequently do not know what levels of performance they are looking for, we have to have means of discovering their latent needs.

Moving onto the area of customization, the organization's attention is again riveted on the customer. Customization options are often expensive to create in a product or service, and if we are to provide them, we must assure that customers will use them. Again it is sometimes misleading to ask customers; they often do not know and exercise customization options only in response to their availability rather than to some deeply felt need they have up to now not been able to articulate.

Finally, as we move into the area of customer service, our focus is on finding ways to ensure that the customer has no wish to exercise the choice of switching to another supplier. To achieve this we must, on the one hand, be able to produce the carrot of consistently excellent service as defined in the customer's terms. We must also seek to raise the switching cost so that the customer is discouraged from pursuing alternative options. To do this we have to know the customer extremely well, probably not as a category of users, but as a series of relationships which at least give the appearance of being individualized.

> *The interesting thing to observe is the move from internal process improvement to external customer focus. What further complicates the sort of overall organizational change the five steps of the quality staircase provide is that we move from problem analysis, standardization and benchmarking – all good hard replicable skills – to the far less concrete area of customer perception, and customer behaviour; which is often intuitive and less predictable in outcome.*

Case Study

The early days of software development required huge ingenuity to produce software applications which were inherently very complex but which would fit within the small memory capacity of the hardware and be contained within the limitations of the operating systems.

Developing word processing software was no mean achievement. The **conformity** standard was an electric typewriter; software that couldn't do what a typewriter could do simply would not be used.

Reliability also proved difficult to achieve, software often crashed losing (as those of us who have been around for a while ruefully remember) hours of work in the process. Electrical fluxes wiped out programmes, floppy discs were savaged by hungry disc drives and so on.

Performance in word processing software started to be achieved when the rich options of fonts and layouts, enabled even ham fisted two finger typists to produce work that looked wonderful. The limitless ability to correct, to change and rehash became a performance advantage which forever differentiated word processing from typing.

Customization in all modern word processing software enables us to design and use our own unique templates, to store and access our data in our own idiosyncratic ways, etc.

Customer focus emerges as the whole software/hardware industry consistently makes their products simpler, easier, more feature rich and flexible. Finally the price/value relationships have improved out of all recognition – another feature of customer focus.

BROADENING THE ORGANIZATION'S INVOLVEMENT – CROSS FUNCTIONALITY

If progressing through the quality staircase involves a shift of vision from inside the organization to a focus on the customer outside it, it also involves a progressively more comprehensive involvement of the components parts of the organization to achieve it.

The environment in which cross functionality is most likely to be successful is one in which the team (if team it is) is genuinely focused on improvement, and not simply on protecting functional turf.

Successful teams depend for their success on working to a clearly articulated and strategically relevant purpose, and on paying great attention to internal team processes which foster co-operation, which inculcate mutual respect, and which adopt the highest standards of honesty and openness.

In the earlier stages we can confine our attentions to the development processes of the product or services; in the later stages, as we move on from reliability, the organization needs much broader cross-functional involvement; no single function of the organization escapes the need for development.

We saw in Chapter 4 some of the downsides of the functionally structured organization. Despite these downsides, a functional basis of organizational structure remains the most frequent form. A journey up the quality staircase will lead fairly soon to the implementation of cross-functional teams – quality circles are a model. The organization will start to compensate for whatever inherent shortcomings exist in structure, it might do so on a short-term assignment basis, or it might initiate permanent cross functionality.

Why this is important is that the environment in which cross functionality is most likely to be successful is one in which the team (if team it is) is genuinely focused on improvement, and not simply on protecting functional turf. Sometimes it happens that functional departments assign people to cross-functional teams for purposes of espionage – keep an eye on what's happening just in case it proves disadvantageous to us. To solve problems, cross-functional teams must behave towards each other with a level of support and respect which is often at variance with the competitive nature of the mature organization.

Successful teams depend for their success firstly on working to a clearly articulated and strategically relevant purpose, and secondly on paying great attention to internal team processes which foster co-operation, which inculcate mutual respect, and which adopt the highest standards of honesty and openness.

A *Kaizen* environment, which is built around the concept of continuous improvement, recognizes the centrality of openness about problems; about preparedness to confront the bad news, about inclusion of all members of the team and about mutual respect and supportiveness. It can flourish in no other environment.

TWO SETS OF VALUES

Western management recognizes, rewards and lionizes results. This naturally needs to competitiveness, striving to achieve the goals, delivering the results, sometimes at great cost. *Kaizen*, on the other hand, accords great recognition to the processes which produce results, to the steps being taken to achieve the goals, to the groundwork being laid towards success. There is a great difference between the values which support these separate points of view. Both in the end are looking for success, arguably *Kaizen* is better able to sustain success over the longer haul.

Western managements tend also to favour rapid, radical and innovative change. When we look at the major management movements in Western organizations over the last decade and a half: delayering, downsizing, outsourcing, process re-engineering, enterprise resource management, etc, their main characteristics are large disruptive one-time initiatives which, when enacted, will change things dramatically and permanently.

The quality staircase model we are dealing with here though is, by its very nature, a gradual, progressive framework which anticipates that incremental improvement and immediate consolidation will work in tandem to deliver the strategic advantage inherent in quality. Most organizations that have addressed the concepts of quality through some of the formal means like ISO9000 for example, have found that it is only through the incremental route, consolidated by compliance to standard that quality is in fact improved and sustained through time.

The quality staircase model we are dealing with here though is, by its very nature, a gradual, progressive framework which anticipates that incremental improvement and immediate consolidation will work in tandem to deliver the strategic advantage inherent in quality.

Indications are, however, that as the pace competition accelerates, driven by ever more demanding customers and ever more global competition, organizations will have to respond more radically, more frequently to their competitive environment. The directors of Toyota, one of the organizations which has used the power of *Kaizen* to achieve enviable international eminence, are using the phrase '. . . *Kaizen* is not enough . . .'. What is not being said here is not that *Kaizen* is no longer relevant – far from it, *Kaizen* remains the core management system of Toyota. Rather what Toyota seems to imply is that the new organization must be able to deliver the disciplines of reliable incremental improvement on the one hand, and the ability to produce high levels of innovation on the other.

> *We are looking at a new strategic capability for all organizations. It is the ability to move up an ever more demanding quality staircase with new definitions of quality which progressively stretch and change the organization, and alter its focus and involve more and more of its functions.*

KEY POINTS

- Quality improvement in products and services, in systems and processes and in customer satisfaction are a necessary precondition for competitive survival.
- To help understand the implications of quality to an organization, a five level scale is devised, the quality staircase.

Figure 9.1   *The quality staircase*

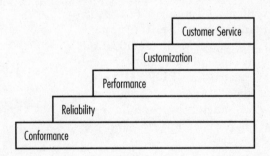

- Most organizations are best able to improve their quality by treating this model as a development track.
- During this development track the organization's attention must switch from an internal focus on systems and procedures to an external focus on customers.
- Also during the development track the organization must become increasingly able to operate cross functionally to deliver the best quality and service.

- Western management, with its focus on results, often finds incremental improvement too slow.

- The successful organizations of the future will be able to manage incremental improvement on the one hand, and increasingly, and speedily enlist an ever-widening range of organizational activities in the delivery of new standards of quality.

Notes

1. *The Global Manufacturing Futures Project* run by the University of Boston, but soliciting input from 12 other international universities and many hundreds of companies is one such organization. Some of their definitions and observations are used in this chapter.

2. Kim, Miller and Heineke 'Mastering the Quality Staircase Step by Step', *Business Horizons* 40 (1).

CHAPTER 10

Introducing Kaizen *to Support a Quality Culture*

Introduction

———

Commitment from the Top

———

Establishing the Purpose

———

The Broad Plan

———

Developing the People Aspects in *Kaizen*

———

Time and Money

———

Some Case Experience

———

Key Points

'There are no short cuts to any place worth going.'
BEVERLEY SILLS, American opera diva

INTRODUCTION

The last chapter made the case for quality and showed how *Kaizen* contributed to helping the organization through the five levels of a quality framework. This chapter focuses on what it is necessary for an organization to do to introduce and install *Kaizen* as a quality-facilitating system.

COMMITMENT FROM THE TOP

Every book you have read, and will ever read about change will tell you that a precondition for enacting far-reaching change in an organization is a demonstrable, consistent and highly visible commitment from the most senior people within the company. This is even more true where the major payback for the change is to develop a quality culture in the organization. Commitment here means more than lip service, it means that the behaviour of all the senior people in the organization consistently supports quality based activities, that decisions taken demonstrably favour quality, and that when quality competes for time or resources, quality wins out.

Almost all manufacturing organizations now conform to one of the major quality standards like ISO 9000 for example. Many service industries are moving in a similar way. Other standards, like Britain's Investors in People or the Business Excellence Model are means employed by managements to institute one form or another of TQM – Total Quality Management. Using one of these standards helps to make public a changed commitment to quality and sometimes it provides a means for positioning the strategic need for the change and helping people within the organization understand its nature.

Commitment also means that the organization will make available the resources to support the change initiative. The resources required are heavily in the area of training, in providing workshops, in developing people's ability to use the basic tools of quality. Resources also need to be devoted to support cross functionality, usually to team building and development, and finally to help recognize and reward achievement.

Chapter 6, *Change and People*, mapped out the role of the change leader; here we will provide a blueprint for introducing *Kaizen* into the organization.

ESTABLISHING THE PURPOSE

Before embarking on a *Kaizen* journey the organization must be absolutely clear about why it is doing so; what it hopes to get out of it, and how it will know that it has succeeded.

Most organizations will introduce *Kaizen* because they are looking to achieve the long-term strategic advantage that arises from three organizational capabilities:

- progressively improving the quality of goods and services
- steadily improving systems and processes within the organization
- consistently improving customer satisfaction.

Before embarking on a Kaizen journey the organization must be absolutely clear about why it is doing so; what it hopes to get out of it, and how it will know that it has succeeded.

Furthermore, most will be doing this on the basis that they require a continuing, systemic ability to achieve these things for the foreseeable future. Organizations are usually looking to do this across all operations to produce the long-term culture change that will permanently sustain *Kaizen* and hence the strategic advantages it provides.

Sometimes *Kaizen* is introduced piecemeal – a particularly intractable set of problems within the organization are 'attacked' with *Kaizen* techniques. This is a possible way of initiating and implementing change but there are two potential dangers.

- *Kaizen* expertise takes time to develop and while it is a set of immediately learnable skills, they improve greatly in effectiveness by prolonged application.
- Much of the sort of problem solving *Kaizen* handles with particular success is achieved by cross-functional involvement. Sometimes it is hard to confine the use of *Kaizen* approaches under these circumstances.

Sometimes variants of *Kaizen* can be introduced in problem-solving mode and, provided the solutions can be consolidated by some form of SDCA, that is no bad thing. Two-day *Kaizen*, described in Chapter 8, is a way of achieving this.

However you handle it, be very clear about what you are getting into and that you have the energy, resources and commitment to sustain the culture change which successful *Kaizen* implementation inevitably produces.

THE BROAD PLAN

Kaizen is such a closely integrated set of philosophies, practices and tools that it is difficult to separate the component parts of it out into a coherent plan for application. The big question is Where do you start? The answers are many and there are a number of ways. The plan which follows is by no means immutable but may provide you with a way in. Essentially it is based on developing expertise in four areas of Kaizen:

- *Kaizen* theory and background thinking
- training people to deal with *Kaizen* in action – particularly at *gemba*
- developing competence in the tools of *Kaizen*
- developing the people related aspects of *Kaizen*.

The plan is summarized in tabular form at the end of the chapter. Each of the major steps is outlined below.

Target the population(s)

You will have to work with at least two separate target populations; the first will be the people at *gemba* – the actual work units you wish to be affected by *Kaizen*. Usually these groups will consist of several existing work units each with a supervisor and a number of operatives. Sometimes you might be putting together one or more first-time teams. More often the work unit suddenly starts to call itself a team.

The second target population is the management structure which supports each work unit. This should involve all the management chain – as high up as you can get.

Where possible the training and development of the two target populations should happen side by side. This is not always an available option, but a shared and developing understanding of *Kaizen* helps orientate both populations. In hierarchical organizations however, it may be better to handle the two populations separately.

Providing the context – usually part of a workshop

Plainly a context for what you are about to try and achieve should be provided for each target population. The most important thing to do here is to show the relationships between the strategic purpose in undertaking this programme, and the changed behaviour which will support the achieving of it. In doing this it often proves valuable to translate purpose into a series of objectives and to help groups establish what these objectives will look like. It is usually premature to try and specify committing objectives at this stage, but agreement on measures and probable time scales usually helps.

*People need more time than one imagines to absorb the implications of **continuous improvement**. The concept of quality as applied to a product or service is usually well understood, moving that concept to embrace processes and customer satisfaction as well needs time to assimilate.*

Getting people up to speed on *Kaizen* theory – usually one or more workshops

People need more time than one imagines to absorb the implications of **continuous improvement.** The concept of quality as applied to a product or service is usually well understood, moving that concept to embrace processes and customer satisfaction as well needs time to assimilate.

What is also difficult to grasp initially is *Kaizen*'s **focus on processes.** Westerners are, as we explored earlier, more usually measured on results, on achieving objectives, on winning. It sometimes takes a while to readjust thinking to accept the underlying *Kaizen* philosophy that results flow out of making the processes first rate. For many people, accepting this has to be an act of faith.

The different approach to job responsibilities, as enshrined in **QCD**, Quality, Cost, Delivery thinking also needs to be dealt with. We outlined this in Chapter 5 when we discussed *Kaizen*'s perception of job responsibilities.

Three other areas of *Kaizen* theory need also to be imparted: *muda* or **waste**, *mura* or **irregularity**, and *muri* or **strain**. Understanding *Kaizen*'s sevenfold definition of waste as being the cost of:

- overproduction
- excess inventory
- repairs and rejects
- wasted motion
- redundant processes
- waiting
- unnecessary transport

... and coupling this with some fundamental thinking about efficient ways of making work flow more easily helps people realize, even in service environments, that there is almost certainly substantial scope for process improvement.

Understanding *Kaizen*'s thinking about **housekeeping**, the Five Ss, also helps people to establish the environment in which *Kaizen* operates and the disciplines on which it relies for success. See Chapter 3 for further information on this. Below are the Japanese originals and two English variants that will help:

Actually enacting the housekeeping tenets of Kaizen *also starts to generate a momentum towards change and to develop the disciplines of good housekeeping.*

Japanese	English 1	English 2 (the Five Cs)
Seiri	Sort	Clear out
Seiton	Straighten	Configure
Seiso	Scrub	Clean and check
Seijitsu	Systematize	Conform
Shisuke	Standardize	Custom and practice

Actually enacting the housekeeping tenets of *Kaizen* also starts to generate a momentum towards change and to develop the disciplines of good housekeeping.

> *Collectively then, this background thinking and experience starts to make* Kaizen *accessible to people and to point out some of the opportunities which exist for improvement.*

> *It also helps in introducing* Kaizen *to an organization that there is*

> *rich case history in each of these background areas to illustrate what can be achieved. Working from* Kaizen *theory through* Kaizen *case history to the work unit's own circumstances starts to generate* Kaizen *consciousness.*

Training people to deal with *Kaizen* in action – ideally mentor-assisted activities, but sometimes one or more workshops

As we expand the thinking and theory about *Kaizen* on the one hand, it is important to make clear to the target populations that *Kaizen* is an intensely practical, pragmatic, low cost system to achieve improvement. The robustness and utility of *Kaizen* must be established early on, and the best way of doing this is to engage in the *gemba* based activities that start to provide practical results.

Understanding and executing a ***Kaizen* story** (see Chapter 8 for an in-depth description) is vital for achieving this. Mentors are especially valuable in helping frame the initial problem, in designing the passage of the 'story', in supervising the **Root Cause Analysis,** deploying the **Five Whys** and in activating the various sequences within the story. In short, taking your target audiences through a *Kaizen* story, perhaps even replicating a *Two-day Kaizen* probably does more to bring alive the realities of *Kaizen* in action than any number of workshops ever achieve.

Much of the depth and significance of *gemba* can be established while the 'story' is being enacted, in particular ideas like **visual management**[1] can be developed. The importance of observation, the immediacy with which corrective action is implemented all emerge from the *Kaizen* story; ideally the process of taking one's target populations through it should not only reveal *Kaizen* in action, it should also solve some real life problems.

If the site of the *Kaizen* story is a production line, much of the substance of **Just-In-Time, Kanban, Productive Maintenance, Set-up Time Reduction** (see Chapter 3) can also be introduced and understood. If the site is not a production line, then the mentor should still be able to introduce these concepts and show their relevance to all work processes.

Gaining competence in the tools of *Kaizen* – training workshops using case study exercises

If *Kaizen* is to flourish in the organization, proficiency in the tools of analysis (the Ishikawa Seven) is very important. Members of the organization must all be able to operate the various tools and must also be aware of which tool to use in order to achieve the most revealing results.

Here is a list of the seven basic tools.

- **Tally charts and check sheets** which are used for data collection and frequency analysis.
- **Pareto diagrams** which illustrate the frequency of occurrence of events and hence establish their relative importance.
- **Fishbone diagrams** are a way of expressing multiple causes and relating them to an overall set of outcomes in a way which enables one to see their contribution.
- **Histograms** are graphic presentations of distribution, usually around a central (bar graphed) peak.
- **Control charts** define acceptable deviations in sequences and thus alert people to deviations from the anticipated.
- **Scatterplots** are diagrams which plot different sets of data against each other so that it is possible to detect relationships between them.
- **Graphs** are a means of expressing data on different axes so that trends, sequences, relationships, etc. can be determined. The entire gamut of graphics is used: line, bar, pie, etc.

If we look at the shift of organizational attention we outlined in the previous chapter as different categories of quality platforms are dealt with, we find that various other forms of analytical tools may be needed as well. Skills in brainstorming, in conducting focus groups, in complex (cross-functional) critical path analysis, in strategic evaluation, etc. may all have to be developed.

Along with these tools the centrality of **PDCA** (Plan, Do, Check, Act) and **SDCA** (Standardize, Do, Check, Act) as, respectively, the analysis and the consolidation routines of continuous improvement must also be rehearsed and embedded within the operating practices of the organization.

DEVELOPING THE PEOPLE ASPECTS
IN *KAIZEN*

For *Kaizen* to operate effectively it must do so in a high trust, high communication, low blame environment. If continuous improvement is the goal, then problems must be recognized, brought to the surface and dealt with. If cross-functional solutions are to be enacted then there is no room for empires to be built. Above all, a receptiveness to change, a willingness to embrace it, and a positive attitude towards it become essential.

For Kaizen *to operate effectively it must do so in a high trust, high communication, low blame environment.*

The team is the principal unit of organization within a *Kaizen* culture. This might simply be the members of a department, the operatives on a given shift, or it might be a cross-functional team put together to fix a problem or set of problems. Accelerating team development so that synergy is achieved faster becomes a way of accelerating the implementation of a *Kaizen* culture.

To implement *Kaizen* team development, programmes need to be undertaken which aim to make participants very clear about the team's purpose, the objectives they are to achieve and the resources they have at their disposal (see Chapter 6). Time has also to be spent on developing the internal processes the team uses. These cover the following.

- The team's **interpersonal skills** – the way they interact with each other on a personal level.

- The team's ability to generate **participation** of all members – people making their own contributions and suggestions as well as their preparedness to accept tasks set by the team.

- The ability of the team to **resolve differences** in a constructive way that does not alienate those who may have held views contrary to the decision taken.

- The **creativity** and imagination the team brings to bear on problem solving and in generating solutions.

- The way in which the team **manages its external relationships** with the rest of the organization.

The evidence is that when teams are handling these internal processes in a satisfactory way, they operate effectively. Empowerment, as we call it in the West, Jishu Kanri – self-management, in Japanese – generally produces exceptional results but needs continuous renewal and support to flourish.

Initiating the morning markets or **morning meetings** (see Chapter 6) also develops successful *Kaizen*. Finally, initiating and nurturing effective **suggestion systems** also contributes to the people development needed for *Kaizen* implementation.

TIME AND MONEY

It takes a long time for an organization to develop a robust *Kaizen* culture, one that can be relied upon to work untiringly at the disciplines of continuous improvement. Once in position however, an organization finds that it is undergoing a consistent level of incremental change, quality and reliability are improving, systems and processes are becoming more effective and customer satisfaction will be on the increase.

The investment is not all long term, however; most organizations will also find that there is immediate and useful payback in the early applications of *Kaizen* tools and systems to solve problems. Some have found that dramatic improvement in efficiency and in cost saving happens very soon – long before a reliable *Kaizen* culture emerges.

Essentially *Kaizen*, though it does use resources of time and opportunity for individual and team development, does not require massive drafts of investment as most major change initiatives do. Much is achieved by the targeted and directed application of common sense, and by unlocking the latent ability of the workforce to improve their surroundings, their processes and their efficiency.

Importantly we find that organizations can develop *Kaizen* capability through a number of routes. Team building and development is first among them, followed closely by interventions to improve organizations' cultural readiness to embrace *Kaizen*.

Some Case Experience

Successful *Kaizen* implementation is usually associated with the production line and with manufacturing. Toyota is probably the world's highest profile *Kaizen* exponents; *Kaizen* is literally its primary management system in all its international plants. It is a mistake to think of *Kaizen* as a technique only used in manufacturing though. As service organizations have increasingly come to the realization that quality and continuous improvement is as germane to them as it is to manufacturing, Kaizen has been more widely applied.

Europe Japan Centre's experience with Kaizen in a Western environment has been in a variety of industries and in a range of applications.

- EJC has worked with the oldest department store in the UK, Voisins in Jersey developing both the top team and teams on the sales floor.

- At Canon EJC has developed cross-functionality, integrating customer service, administration and sales activities in the pursuit of enhanced customer satisfaction.

- At Cox Pharmaceuticals[2] an ongoing programme thrives. It originally started in a packaging division of Cox and has gone on to develop a wide range of team-centred activities.

- EJC worked with SAJ, the largest Malaysian utility, to develop its *Kaizen* capability as the organization dealt with deregulation. Organizational culture audits were undertaken and communications systems were enhanced to facilitate the application of *Kaizen*.

- At Norris Seal, a specialist engineering company in Houston EJC again worked with the top team to improve the cultural climate necessary to support their *Kaizen* initiatives.

- Kaizen techniques have been extensively used in the quality programmes in the Consumer Finance Division of TSB Homeloans with spectacularly successful results.

KEY POINTS

Step 1. Gain commitment from the top of the company downwards.

Step 2. Establish the strategic purpose the organization is trying to achieve.

Step 3. Select the populations – work units and the management which support each.

Step 4. Institute the following programme . . .

Need	Purpose	Media for delivery	Content
Provide the context	People must understand the relationship between the strategic purpose the company is trying to achieve and the behaviour, which is in their gift, to support it.	Usually a facilitated workshop	Establish team purpose. Consider probable objectives. Devise the metrics . . . how will we know?
Develop *Kaizen* theory	• To understand the core thinking behind continuous improvement and *Kaizen*. • To have a 'philosophy' against which to judge what they do.	Facilitated workshops using: • direct teaching • case study • live example in the organization.	• The implications of continuous improvement • Focus on process • QCD – quality, cost, delivery • *Muda, mura* and *muri* • The seven Ss of housekeeping.
Kaizen in action	To show the application of the theory in real problem solving. Actually solve problems	Mentor assisted activity: • as far as possible at *gemba* • assisted by workshops where needed.	• *Kaizen* story • Root cause analysis • Five Whys • Visual management • JIT/*kanban* • Productive maintenance
Competence in *Kaizen* tools	To be able to use the appropriate analytical tool to facilitate root cause analysis.	Facilitated workshops: • taught examples • case studies • assignments.	• Tally charts • Pareto • Fishbone • Histograms • Control charts • Scatterplots • Graphs • PDCA/SDCA

Need	Purpose	Media for delivery	Content
People aspects of *Kaizen*	• To achieve long lasting culture change. • To accelerate team development. • To generate company wide suggestions system.	• Facilitated team meetings • Team development activities	• Interpersonal skills • Participation • Resolution of differences • Creativity • Managing external relationships • Conducting morning meetings • Suggestion systems

Notes

1. Visual management is an important *Kaizen* technique. Not only does it stress the need for observation at *gemba*, it also advocates that key performance results be publicly displayed, annotated, made simple and easily comprehensible to everyone at *gemba*.

2. The experience of Cox Pharmaceuticals is well reported in *Kaizen Strategies for Improving Team Performance* published by Financial Times Prentice Hall.

CHAPTER 11

Causes and Implications of Major Changes in Organizations

'Anything in history or nature that can be described as changing steadily can be seen as heading toward catastrophe.'

SUSAN SONTAG (b. 1933) American essayist

INTRODUCTION

We have touched several times in this book on the evolution versus revolution debate. We have painted *Kaizen* as the management system which provides the organization with the means of strategic evolution because of its ability to improve continuously the quality of goods and services, the processes by which the organization operates and customer satisfaction. In an environment of gradual change these evolutionary organizational competencies are not only desirable, they are essential.

Gradual change can no longer be relied upon, however, and the history of many, if not most, organizations is that periods of gradual change, evolution, are interspersed with periods of dramatic change, revolution if you like. It is further true that, when confronted with dramatic change, organizations, even very efficient ones, do not necessarily adapt effectively.

Between 1990 and 1993, IBM, a company which had dominated the computer industry worldwide, the largest and most influential player in the industry, lost $14 billion dollars! The trigger that caused this catastrophe was the PC; IBM was late into the market, unable to change its measured pace, unaccustomed to its competitive position being seriously challenged.

Credit Lyonnais in France, once Europe's largest bank, proved itself incapable of adapting to the revolutionary changes in competitive climate following financial deregulation. Between 1994 and 1998 the bank was technically bankrupt and saved from receivership only by the intervention of the French State. The cost was a staggering $25 billion dollars before Credit Lyonnais returned to profit,

Kaizen provides the organization with the means of strategic evolution because of its ability to improve continuously the quality of goods and services, the processes by which the organization operates and customer satisfaction. In an environment of gradual change these evolutionary organizational competencies are not only desirable, they are essential.

making a mere $176 million in 1998. On the strength of this it is to be privatized, the French State selling most of its 88 per cent shareholding in the company.

> *It is sobering to find in research conducted by Shell that of the 1970 Fortune 500 companies, one third had ceased to exist by 1983.*

The question arises as to whether patterns are discernible. Are there ways in which an organization can know when its strategy is most sensibly focused in the areas of evolution and continuous improvement, or when its strategy should more appropriately pursue a route of radical change?

CONTINUOUS ENVIRONMENTAL CHANGE

Change is happening all the time, sometimes we realize the extent of it only by looking backwards and thinking about how we have been affected by it. Change is an ongoing process and we adapt to it constantly and without great effort. Such change we can call 'continuous' because what is changing is relatively consistent with what has happened before, a development or an extension rather than a radical redefinition of things.

Let us suppose that this is the 'usual' condition in which organizations operate. The strategy organizations employ in relatively stable markets is based on continuity as we have defined it above. These are markets which are not being affected by a high degree of technological change, nor by major changes in the product or service being provided, and markets which are not the subject of major legislative change such as deregulation for example.

These relatively calm periods of continuous change often follow periods when there has been great turbulence and disorder in the market. In the early days of the PC, for example, competition was based on operating systems: Apple Mac, IBM's OS/2 and Microsoft's Windows. As long as no standard dominated, the competitive environment was risky; for the three major system contenders the stakes for success or failure were high. For the customer, making the 'wrong' choice had risk and potential cost attached to it.

With the adoption of Windows as virtually the standard system, the competitive environment settled down. Competition became based on the features of the hardware and the radical differentiation that had existed because of three different operating systems was now reduced to competing on price, on availability, on delivery times, on

---

Case Study

In the UK at the time of writing the food retailing business represents a relatively continuous and stable competitive environment. Three or four major suppliers, Tesco, Sainsbury, Asda and Safeway dominate the market. All offer relatively indistinguishable services and virtually identical value for money.

Competition is very intense, however, and the battle for market share goes on all the time. An advertising campaign can have a significant effect, positive or negative. Customer loyalty is a key area of competition and each competitor offers loyalty cards, incentive systems, shopping aids and so on.

The system is stable and while criteria for success and the winning of market share do change, essentially the arena for competition is well defined.

---

memory capacity, etc. None of these competitive advantages is long-lived and competitors jockey to excel in one or more of them simultaneously.

There are a number of industries where the rate of change is paced more by the ingenuity of competitors than by any fundamental underlying shift in the environment. The oil industry is an example, so are most utilities, post privatization, and so is most banking post financial deregulation.

Characteristic of this environment is the need for the organization to provide increasing levels of quality, improved levels of service, and stable or falling prices, all those benefits which *Kaizen* can and does deliver.

Organizations are, of course, not secure in these periods of continuous change. Competition is usually intense, price pressure is often acute, and margins are sometimes under pressure.

> *There are a number of industries where the rate of change is paced more by the ingenuity of competitors than by any fundamental underlying shift in the environment.*

It is an interesting statement on the speed and unpredictability of change that the three paragraphs in the case study above were written in late spring 1999. By early summer 1999 the announcement of the acquisition of ASDA by Walmart looks as if it may redefine this competitive environment. The British Government's investigations of supermarket pricing may also have a radical effect.

Some organizations are gaining market share, and some are losing it. Competitive advantage is usually short-lived and organizations find themselves gaining, losing and then regaining share once more.

DISCONTINUOUS ENVIRONMENTAL CHANGE

This occurs when the competitive environment undergoes some radical form of change. It is called 'discontinuous' because what characterizes it is not an extension of what has happened before, not a natural development, not an anticipated change. Often this sort of change is technologically based, sometimes it is presaged by a change in the law, and sometimes it occurs for quite other reasons.

Examples of technological change abound. Aeroplanes replaced ships and trains as the major means of moving people about. PCs replaced typewriters, CDs replaced tapes which replaced LP records, e-mail progressively replaces faxes which replaced postage and so on.

Changes in the law may produce discontinuous change and have far reaching effects. Financial deregulation is an example within many people's memory. Privatization of utilities is another example. Much anti-trust legislation has had considerable impact on the competitive environment as, for example, the break up of AT&T into various MiniBells. The large international trade agreements like GATT have an effect on the movement of goods and services which can make radical differences in countries which have sheltered behind protectionism. European Union legislation affects competition in major ways.

In the area of 'other reasons' lie a number of events which have intruded to make for revolutionary change. The opening of the Channel Tunnel, for example, radically changed the economy of the Port of Dover which planned for a reduction in revenue of 75 per cent within a single year. It also changed the competitive basis of the ferry companies which operate ships between England and France, leading to a merger between two of the three competing operators.

The fall of the Berlin Wall, ending the cold war, has had a radical effect on the whole US defence industry, with statistics suggesting that of the 120,000 companies which once supplied the US Department of Defense, only one quarter of that number now do so. Of the fifteen top suppliers in 1990, there are now four.

At a more insidious level, the effects of globalization also intrude in a major way. The collapse of the currencies of the Pacific Rim in the

Case Study

In his memorably entitled book *Only the Paranoid Survive*, Andy Grove,[1] the former CEO of Intel, the world's largest chip manufacturer, tells of two cases where Intel confronted events which may have changed the nature of the company. The first of these did, the second did not.

For the first 15 years of its life, Intel was in the business of engineering computer memory. By the mid 1980s the company found itself under increasing pressure from Japanese competitors. Intel saw its margins shrinking as it responded to an increasingly disabling price war.

The company started to switch its resources and manufacturing capacity to microprocessor technology which is, as we now know, the hallmark of Intel's success. The transition took two years, during which time Grove reports on the dissonance the organization felt. The company saw itself as a world leader in memory, it talked about itself in this light, but increasingly its behaviour was otherwise. It was only when it had virtually accomplished the switch of focus to microprocessors that it could relinquish the rhetoric of the memory product lines and talk about itself as a dominant microprocessor manufacturer.

The other major area which the company viewed as a potential 'strategic inflection point' (the phrase Grove uses to describe one of these major change triggers) was associated not with competitive pressure but with technological change. RISC (Reduced Instruction Set Computing) was widely believed in the industry to be the coming technology for microprocessors. Half of Intel agreed, half disagreed. The company asked itself whether it could pursue both options and decided that it could not; in either case it would be devoting only half its resources to the right answer, and wasting half its resources on the wrong bet.

In the event the company pulled out of developing RISC technology and this proved to be the correct decision.

Grove offers an excellent analogy in his 1997 Stockton Lecture;[2] he is dealing with the difficulty in recognizing at any one time whether an event is merely transitory, an element of continuous change, or whether it is a strategic inflection point, the precursor to discontinuous change. His analogy is an electrical system in which there is inevitably noise. Is it merely 'noise' that need not be taken seriously, or is it a signal, in which case a response is required.

To differentiate, he offers the rule of the single silver bullet – in a competitive shoot-out you have only one shot. If you choose your major competitor as the target, there is probably simply noise in the system. If you choose somebody else, you have probably isolated the source of a strategic inflection point, somebody hatching a discontinuous change.

late 1990s alters the labour cost components of goods and services in a way which redefines the manufacturing sourcing decisions of major brands.

THE DISCONTINUITIES ABOUND

In Chapter 1, we spoke of the factors that were driving change in the contemporary operating climate. We isolated demanding customers, globalization, technology, the broader accountability of organizations, and the way people are changing as the major drivers. The combined effect of these seems not to produce an environment of sustained discontinuity, but rather that the periods of continuous change, the flat pieces between the peaks, are shorter.

At the heart of the operating environment at the turn of the century is the Internet, which is having and will continue to have the most profound effect on the way organizations conduct themselves.

It must also be said that at the heart of the operating environment at the turn of the century is the Internet, an entity which is having and will continue to have the most profound effect on the way organizations conduct themselves. It is affecting and will continue to affect the way in which markets are organized, the way in which goods and services are delivered, and the way in which customers interact with their suppliers. It will also have its effect very fast.

The heart of the computer industry really started to beat with the invention of the transistor in 1948; in the second half of the twentieth century computers have transformed our lives and the way we do business. It will take far less time for the Internet to have an even more radical effect than the computer. We are, in short, in the middle of a period of major discontinuity because of the Internet.

> **In summary then** it is plain that the successful organization has to cultivate the strategies of continuous improvement as delivered by Kaizen. It has also to be alert to the potential for major change emerging from technology, legislation or simply events. There always exists the possibility that at short notice the organization will need to initiate a major change to respond to an environmental development that poses a serious strategic threat.

If this is the environment in which the modern organization must survive, then it reasonable to suggest that a new style of organization is needed. In the next chapter we outline some of the characteristics of the responsive organization, an organization designed to thrive in a modern competitive climate.

KEY POINTS

- Change is of two kinds: continuous environmental change and discontinuous change.
- Continuous change is consistent with the immediate past.
- Continuous change requires a company strategy which can be delivered by *Kaizen*.
- Discontinuous change occurs when some radical, largely unanticipated redefinition of the environment occurs.
- Discontinuous change arises usually from:
  - technological advance
  - legislation
  - 'other' reasons.
- Discontinuous change happens more frequently and the intervals of continuous change are getting shorter.
- The Internet is an, as yet unquantified, discontinuity.
- A new style of organization, the responsive organization, is needed if an organization is to thrive in the new competitive climate.

Notes

1. Grove, A. (1998) *Only the Paranoid Survive*, HarperCollins.
2. Grove, A. (1997) 'Navigating Strategic Inflection Points', *Business Strategy Review* 8 (3).

CHAPTER 12

The Responsive Organization –
a Vehicle for Continuous Change

'Who in the same given time can produce more than others has vigour; who can produce more and better, has talents; who can produce what none else can, has genius.'

JOHANN KASPAR LAVATER (1741–1801), Swiss divine

INTRODUCTION

The responsive organization is one that can successfully deal with the continuous change necessary to survive in a competitive climate.

The responsive organization is one that can successfully deal with the continuous change necessary to survive in a competitive climate. On the one hand it must have the discipline and competence to work at continuous improvement of products and services, internal processes and customer satisfaction. On the other hand it must be capable of responding to changes in its operating environment, and doing so quickly. For many, these requirements produce a vision of irreconcilable paradoxes.

On the one hand we want ...	On the other hand we need ...
• Continuous incremental improvement	• Breakthrough, re-invention
• Consistency of performance/ output	• Diversity and range of operations
• The disciplines of TQM	• Creativity and inventiveness
• Focus on process	• Focus on external environment
• Conformity to standards	• Creativity and inventiveness
• Reward for team success	• Reward for individual entrepreneurship
• People empowered to get on with things	• People empowered to step outside of established procedures.

Now we can take the view that these two sets of requirements are clustered at opposite ends of a spectrum of behaviour and that each represents a choice, which excludes the other end of the spectrum. Or we can set ourselves the task of having it all and creating the responsive organization. The reality is that unless yours is an extremely stable monopolist activity, unaccountable to shareholders, not the subject of impending legislation and insulated from technological advance, you have no choice but to try and build the responsive organization.

As we define this new style of organization through the rest of this chapter, you will encounter information introduced earlier in this book. To the extent that these concepts facilitate organizational flexibility and versatility, they are repeated here.

WHAT A RESPONSIVE ORGANIZATION LOOKS LIKE

Here is a diagram which illustrates the concept.

Figure 12.1 *A responsive organization*

Core organizational systems	Components of the systems	Orientation provided to the people
Directional systems	Purpose Vision Values	Deals with why we are here and where we are going
Control systems	Organizational culture Strategy	Deals with how we are going to get there
Operating systems	Work processes Organizational structure Hierarchy People management systems	Deals with what you expect me to do

The divisions above are, of course, entirely arbitrary and simply devised to make explanation and description easier. The fact that people management systems is listed as the last component needs also to be flagged. As we have said earlier, the degree to which people will enable change to take place represents the sum total of the organization's ability to enact it. In fact the entire model above is designed to enable people to operate in the organization with precision and confidence.

> *The degree to which people will enable change to take place represents the sum total of the organization's ability to enact it.*

The model uses shading rather than lines to separate the core organizational systems. This is meant to show that the systems blend into each other and are not really separate rooms with doors to go through. Rather each affects the other, and while the emphasis changes as one moves from one core set of systems to the next, the overall effect is cumulative rather than discrete.

Let us examine the responsive organization in greater detail.

DIRECTIONAL SYSTEMS – WHY WE ARE HERE AND WHERE WE ARE GOING

Achieving a common shared and intimate understanding of the directional systems of the organization, purpose, vision and values, is the essential precondition to achieving organizational versatility. Without it the organization is unable to provide context, relevance, meaning or reason to the jobs of individuals. Without it strategy cannot be defined, and without a strategy, the organization will be working to tactical plans only; it may win a few battles, but it will certainly be losing the war.

The context or orientation the various directional components provide the organization are these.

- Purpose describes what we are here to do.
- Vision describes where we are going.
- Values describe the overarching rules by which we will conduct ourselves in achieving the above.

Clarifying, refining, and agreeing these things is the means by which the organization lays down its main directional course, the primary navigational line along which it will travel.

To be effective, everyone in the organization must understand these components, and the process of establishing them, debating them, exploring them and agreeing them must be repeated in microcosm for each operating unit. To ensure that the organization is pulling in the same direction in all its component parts, time must also be spent to reflect on and define the purpose of each of the operating units so that they all support, amplify and enable the overall organizational direction. Without this commonality of understanding, and without the alignment it brings, chaos starts to creep in.

Purpose

In the seventies organizations spent time developing mission statements. These were mostly treated as file-and-forget documents, and despite the considerable amount of time spent in developing them and the energy spent in nailing them to the office walls, they had very little effect.

Modern thinking concentrates on the purpose of the organization and really tries to focus on what the organization provides that constitutes its unique reason for existence. This is very different in concept from the all-purpose, leave-nobody-out, cover-every-angle approach of the mission statements.

The process of developing purpose sidesteps the issue of the organization's need to make money; it takes that as read. There is far greater value in identifying the particular benefits the organization provides to its clients. Focusing on this should also circumvent discussions on the product or service being offered because this is merely the way the organization is going about providing the customer benefit at the time of asking. If it is serious about purpose, the organization will seek to provide those benefits by other means and by other products or services should the customer require it.

As outlined above, each of the operating units must develop its own purpose as well. Each must be a subset of, and enabler for, the main organizational purpose. To be effective and to contribute to organizational versatility, the exercise of determining purpose must be given time, allocated importance, and taken seriously.

'Are we on purpose?' should be a powerful question, asked often and treated with respect.

Case Experience

In my own work on purpose with organizations, I have never found even the most senior people to be in agreement about purpose. There is always an area of common understanding, but there is also always a debate as to the extent or reach of the purpose.

To prevent the mistakes of the old mission statement exercise, I always urge clients to write the purpose down, but to promise never to use it in its written form. The need is to talk about it, to describe it, to communicate it at every level and in very precise detail. If people merely read it, the import of it may well be lost, the precision of it will certainly be.

Vision

If the pursuit of purpose is the main contextual reference for the organization, then vision defines and describes the destination for which it is aiming. Vision, to be effective, must be aspirational but achievable. People are not set alight by pedestrian goals, which are arrived at by extrapolation. Equally they are frustrated by unrealistic expectations.

Vision, to be effective, must be aspirational but achievable.

The components of vision are usually fairly numerous. Typically they will cover some comparative or actual financial targets. They will usually specify some form of growth which might be defined as market share or competitive ranking. They will usually address quality, efficiency and customer satisfaction criteria. They may do this by recourse to current measures, or they may simply specify an aspiration for which a measure will need to be defined. Finally, the vision will also try to specify some sort of measure of staff competence, staff satisfaction and other employee related criteria.

Developing vision can usefully be achieved by using the Kaplan and Norton balanced scorecard.[1] Here four major categories of measures are defined:

- financial measures
- internal business process measures

- learning and growth measures for staff
- customer related measures.

What goes into each category depends entirely on the organization. Experience shows that organizations can usually specify very easily those things they feel it is important to measure. As with establishing purpose, however, it often requires time and patient debate to agree the actual measures which will define the vision.

It is also often the case as the vision is developed that precise measures are not specified in the sense that they can become quantifiable organizational objectives. It is perfectly acceptable to define orders of performance or even relative changes in performance without committing to an objective until some proper thought and investigation can define and specify it.

Defining vision must then be cascaded down the organization with each operating unit's vision a subset of and contributor to the overall corporate vision. Whether one uses the balanced scorecard or not, the cascade activity must take place in order to provide the directional pull at all organizational levels.

Values

To provide orientation and guidance for employees, a series of parameters is needed which broadly specifies what the organization considers important. Values are different from both purpose and vision because they describe the ethical constraints within which the organization chooses to conduct itself. An organization's values are, of course, additional to the legal and professional obligations by which every organization is expected to conduct itself.

In Chapter 1 we mentioned the concept of organizational accountability, i.e. the fact that the modern business operates at the centre of a web of responsibilities and must decide how it wishes to deal with each component of its environment.

In their work on the company of the future[2] the Royal Society of Arts postulates the concept of a 'licence to operate'. The view is that organizations are successful to the extent that they can balance the interests of the entities in the operating environment that affect them. Such entities might be:

- The law and the regulators
- The reputation of the industry
- Pressure groups
- Political opinion

- Industry and market standards
- The media
- Public opinions and confidence
- Individual attitudes; customers, suppliers, investors, the community, etc.

When an organization establishes the values by which it wants to conduct itself, it has to ask itself how it would like each of these entities to regard it. Most importantly, in all its transactions with its environment, it must be consistent in applying the values that it has decided to espouse. If it is to do this, then its employees, in whose hands most of these transactions rest, must be able to act with certainty and assurance. To a limited extent this can be controlled by policies and procedures; in the fast moving modern operating climate it is more efficiently achieved by the organization sharing, understanding, respecting and applying a common set of values.

As with purpose and vision, the values of the organization must be established with a wide involvement of all its members. Establishing values is not, and should not be, a democratic debate. The most senior people in the organization must have a strong view of values and the cascading or consultative exercise that must be undertaken should be designed to have these values percolate through the organization and, more importantly, everybody must understand their implications.

Publishing a list of the organization's values will have as much effect as the old fashioned mission statements we discussed above: file-and-forget. So what is needed is an internal communications strategy which helps people understand the values and their importance in affecting what people in the organization choose to do and how they choose to do it. Workshops are the classic ways of achieving this, but much more effective in cementing values into the organization is the degree to which everybody, but especially the most visible and senior people, are seen to support the values and conduct themselves in a manner consistent with them. See *Culture* below.

Case Study

Among the problems that the responsive organization sometimes confronts is the potential conflict between total quality approaches and values.

The newly appointed Managing Director of one of London's major airports inherited a mature TQM programme when he took on the job. Regular and comprehensive reports landed on his desk reporting on quality advances in a number of areas; in fact in every area you could think of. When he received a report on quality improvements to the airport's potted plants he felt that things had gone too far and that it was time to intervene and lay down some new ground rules about what was important around here.

His view was that the primary and overarching value of the airport must be safety and he was concerned that the TQM programme was deflecting energy and concentration away from this essential responsibility that must be felt by everybody who worked there. A new set of values was drawn up to re-channel the activities of his very large staff into the combined areas of safety and customer service, with the unambiguous understanding that in cases of conflict safety prevailed.

Values tend to change little over time in effective organizations, they remain a fairly constant backdrop against which changing strategies and changing operating procedures can be reliably enacted. To some extent they become key to longer-term strategy because some organizations use values as part of their differentiation. For example, Body Shop's strong environmental values help mark it out as different from other cosmetic suppliers and these values appear to drive much of the company's strategy and certainly its operations.

> *It is fair to say that at the heart of Kaizen lie a set of values that many organizations find appropriate in the support they offer to purpose and vision (to say nothing of the robust implementation they can provide for strategy). The following are among these values.*
>
> - *The belief that everything is capable of improvement.*
> - *The disciplines of 'speaking with data', that is, gathering information to establish root causes for dysfunction.*

- *The belief that it is at* gemba, *the place where the work happens, the heart of the process, that effective, low cost, common-sense improvements can invariably be made.*

- *The openness with which problems are brought to the surface, confronted and solved – there is an honesty and lack of concealment here which, when it operates at a high level of efficiency in an organization, is a powerful competitive advantage.*

THE CONTROL SYSTEMS – HOW WE ARE GOING TO GET THERE

The directional systems of purpose, vision and values tend to change little over time, and it is through the use of the organization's control systems, culture and strategy, that the steering, the navigation and the detail of the organizational journey is controlled in the responsive organization.

Culture

Culture, as we have said elsewhere, is the sum total of the belief systems which the employees hold in the organization. It is a clear, and usually very accurate, perception of what is REALLY important around here. No matter what the organization says, no matter what its chief executive says, no matter what my manager says, certain things can be readily predicted. In given circumstances the organization will behave in certain ways. Staff can predict what will be rewarded, what punished and what ignored.

Culture, while not immutable, does not change fast, this is because it is established by observation. If employees observe a cause-effect relationship of significance, it starts to affect their belief systems. If it is observed to apply consistently, it becomes part of the organizational culture. It starts to affect the employees' behaviour to the extent that they will avoid the punishment, if punishment it is, or they seek the reward, if reward it is, in the cause-effect sequence. The behavioural consequences produced by consistently observed phenomena are a major source of the motive power behind the organization's day-to-day activity.

It can readily be seen that purpose, vision and values, all start to lay the foundation of the organization's culture and day-to-day observations start to refine this foundation into a set of operating criteria for each employee.

It can readily be seen that purpose, vision and values, all start to lay the foundation of the organization's culture and day-to-day observations start to refine this foundation into a set of operating criteria for each employee.

Successful organizations, especially those that dominate a market for a period of time, tend to develop a culture of great confidence. Achieving success reinforces the way the organization is behaving. During a period of growth and high performance, cultural norms grow up which, because they consistently succeed, become uncriticized exemplars of how to do it right. Organizations and their employees become very good at replicating and refining the success patterns.

When the organization hits some fundamental environmental change it is often that culture of success which makes it most difficult for the organization to enact change. IBM dismissed the significance of the PC because of the success of its huge installed mainframe business base. GM 'knew its customers so well' that it felt confident in ignoring Japanese compacts as a transient fashion.

Nissan has billions of dollars of accumulated debt at the time this book is being written. A partial acquisition by Renault, a company a fraction of Nissan's size has recently been announced. Yukata Kume, President of Nissan is credited with saying when he took office that the most difficult task he faced was to reform the corporate culture; he is reputed to have said: '…the major reason for our suffering in our business predicament lay within Nissan itself'.[3]

It is plain that a culture which has the confidence and assurance to replicate its successes must also have the ability to spot that the fact that the game has changed, and have the humility to change fast, sometimes abandoning the hard learned lessons of former success.

The advantages that a *Kaizen* based culture offers lie in:

- the acceptance that change is continuous and ongoing
- the belief that improving the processes for which I am responsible is as much a part of my job as producing output from those processes
- the attitude that enacting change is not another chore, but an expected activity
- the acceptance that the tried-and-tested is merely the current standard and that the standard will move on.

The potential disadvantages of a *Kaizen* culture lie in:

- the belief that change is always incremental
- Too great an internal focus (the process) and too little on the outside world (the competitor)
- a possible over-emphasis on consensus, rather than leading change.

Strategy

Strategy is the most important control system of the organization. Essentially this is its plan for long-term survival and growth. If we clearly understand and share purpose, vision and values, if we have developed a culture that supports these things, then we also need to know:

- what products or services we are providing
- to whom they are being provided
- the basis of our differentiation from competitors
- how we are physically going to do this
- how we are going to fund it.

Chapter 2 talks at some length about strategy and shows how *Kaizen* and a planning system called *hoshin kanri* can be used in tandem to develop a shared understanding of the organization's strategy, while at the same time supporting the need for incremental change and break-through.

Whatever model the organization uses, the internalization of the strategy by all employees is vital to the dynamics of the responsive organization. The behaviour of employees in support of the strategy and consistent with the purpose, the vision and the values can only be ensured if there is a deep understanding of what the organization is trying to achieve.

There is simply no substitute for broad involvement of the entire workforce in developing and implementing strategy.

In my experience this can only be gained if employees, at all levels, have been involved in the development of the strategy. If a precondition of achieving responsiveness is the way the information cascades down the company, then equally the capillarity system, the way in which information flows upwards, must be just as efficient. There is simply no substitute for broad involvement of the entire workforce in developing and implementing strategy.

THE ESSENCE OF THE RESPONSIVE ORGANIZATION

To this point the description of the responsive organization is focused on getting alignment and deep understanding through it. Success rests on two parallel analogies that we at the Europe Japan Centre incorporated into our book on Kaizen Teams[4] *but which, for completeness of understanding we need to repeat here.*

- *An aligned organization is a fractal system,[5] a system in which the same geometrical pattern is repeated at ever reducing scales throughout it. (A cauliflower is a fractal system with each floret a smaller version of the total cauliflower.) In other words, the nature and essence of the organization is reproduced identically at all levels within the organization in the same form.*

- *The other great analogy stems from the much older work of George Ainsworth Land who likened the aligned organization to the human body. Each cell contains a perfect and complete set of DNA (purpose, vision, values and culture). While the functional specificity of each cell is different, each is part of the host organism and capable of producing that organism's unique characteristics.*

THE OPERATING SYSTEMS – WHAT YOU EXPECT ME TO DO

The operating systems of the responsive organization must have a single principle guiding them; they must enable it to fulfil its strategy. Chapter 2 outlines the core thinking behind this, and each of the four categories of operating systems, which we have earlier called the 'levers of change' has to make its contribution to effectiveness.

For a more detailed description of the scope presented by each of the components of operating system see the relevant chapter (3–6), here we summarize the characteristics of each of these systems which are usually found in the responsive organization.

Operating system or change lever	Characteristics in the responsive organization
Work processes	• *Kaizen* or some form of *Kaizen* approach is usual. This embraces the means to focus on: – improvement of processes – reduction in process cost – reduction in waste – improvement in quality of output – the customer as the next stage in the process. • Usually contain little redundancy or duplication of effort. • Undergoing a relative constant degree of change. • Internal processes are often linked upstream to supplier input and downstream to customers (JIT inventory levels, joint component design and specification, etc.) • Appropriate IT support systems.
Organizational structure	• Structure is simple and transparent. • Organizations are decentralized with smaller operating units. • Teams are almost always an important structural component.

Operating system or change lever	Characteristics in the responsive organization
	• The organization is built to enhance core organizational competencies, i.e. non-core is outsourced.
	• Designed to balance functional expertise and cross-functional effectiveness.
	• Ability to co-ordinate multiple relationships (partners, suppliers, part-timers, etc.).
	• Far greater use of formal and informal networks.
	• Enable good focus on the customer.
	• Enable good focus on the competitor.
Organizational hierarchy	• Flatter, few levels between CEO and worker.
	• Excellent bi-directional information flow (networks).
	• Developed decision making – close to the problem as possible – the *Kaizen* supervisor model.
	• Purpose, vision and values-driven decision making.

	• Management focused less on control and more on:
	  – defining the boundaries of operations,
	  – assuring the understanding of Purpose, Vision, Values and Strategy
	  – modelling the cultural norms.

People management systems	• Skilled, multi-tasking capability. • Individuals able to articulate relationship between their job and strategy.
	• Training and development needs assessed and being dealt with.
	• A good objectives system; relevance to strategy, transparent.
	• Individuals are the recipients of consistent, accurate and frequent feedback.
	• Participation systems (teams, morning markets, suggestion schemes, small group participation).
	• Rewards tied to achievement.
	• Individuals have positive perception of organization and manager.

Case Study

This move to build more responsive organizations is gaining momentum and during the last decade of the millennium it is probably responsible for a great deal of organizational change. The Harris Association organization conducted a poll for A.T. Kearny,[6] the management consultancy subsidiary of EDS, which shows some startling similarities among 100 international corporations.

- At the start of the decade 47 per cent of surveyed organizations were decentralized, five years later 64 per cent had adopted decentralized structures.
- Of the decentralized organizations many are structured on a product directed basis. Even those organizations which are not decentralized, 55 per cent (up from 25 per cent five years previously) favour product directed structures as distinct from process or functional structures.
- Three quarters of surveyed organizations rely on team-based operating units.
- 83 per cent of organizations surveyed have undergone some form of process re-engineering which is generally regarded as having been successful. It is fair to point out that since this survey, Business Process Re-engineering has generally been on the decline.

A.T. Kearney's own investigations of ten top multinationals including ABB, Electrolux, Ford, Motorola, Shell, Texas Instruments and Volvo show the following trends.

- Organizations are focusing on being driven by customers and by reducing cost.
- Decision making is moving down the organization.
- Cross-functional teams are on the increase.
- Leadership has become increasingly a business of setting the purpose, vision and values and leading by example (modelling the desired culture).

SO WHAT . . .?

So now, you have a clear idea of what the responsive organization looks like, how best to organize and some of the things that you need to do to make it work. Of itself the changes you would probably have to make to transform your organization into a responsive organization are likely to be far reaching. It seems to me that you are well entitled to the 'so what . . .?' question: what will it give you that you did not have before, and above all how does it help with change?

Here is my best shot at a reply.

Change in most Western management environments is a series of cataclysmic events where the organization has to be stopped doing A and started doing B. Disruption, cynicism, accusations of flavour-of-the-day, unlearning and relearning, are all characteristics of this approach.

The responsive organization, with its clear sense of direction, its smaller operating units, its devolved decision making and its strong outward focus on its environment undergoes relatively fewer cataclysmic changes. It is responsive because it automatically adjusts to changes in its environment and adapts itself with precision and reliability.

The responsive organization is less in need of the intervention from the organization's centre and where this has to occur because of a change in the game, it is far more robust in adapting to a revised definition of direction than those organizations which have to be substantially demolished and then reconstructed.

> *The reason that* Kaizen *can make so strong a contribution is because of the cultural norms it provides, the discipline its instils and the tools it uses.* Kaizen's *focus on process, what happens inside, is replicated in the responsive organization by a matching ability to focus outside.*

KEY POINTS

- A responsive organization is able both to institutionalize incremental improvement and at the same time respond quickly to a swiftly changing environment.
- It is characterized by concentrating on gaining alignment among its employees, particularly in the areas of purpose, vision and values.

- It develops a strong positive culture by the way it models rather than decrees the cultural norms it espouses.

- It takes care to develop its strategy with a high degree of involvement so that the strategy is perfectly understood at all levels in the organization.

- It organizes itself in a way which best enables the implementation of strategy.

- Work processes are built round core competencies the organization needs.

- Structurally it operates with smaller, more focused units.

- Hierarchically it is flatter with devolved decision making and management spending more time on gaining alignment rather than controlling.

- People are multi-skilled, developed and involved.

- *Kaizen* helps by providing the internal disciplines which need to be matched with the same quality of external focus.

Notes

1. Kaplan and Norton (1996) *The Balanced Scorecard*, Harvard Business School Press.

2. RSA Inquiry (1995) *Tomorrow's Company*, Royal Society of Arts.

3. Kotter and Rothbard (1993) *Cultural Change at Nissan Motors*, Harvard Business School Case 9-491-079.

4. Colenso, M. (ed.) (1999) *Kaizen Strategies for Improving Team Performance*, Financial Times Prentice Hall.

5. This stems from work by Roger Putt shortly to be published in his book called *The Builder Binder* due for publication in autumn 1999.

6. Harrison, D.B. (1995) 'Shaping the organization of the future', *Canadian Business Review* 22 (4).

CHAPTER 13

Why Change Goes Wrong and What to Do About It

'Mistakes are a fact of life. It is the response to error that counts.'
NIKKI GIOVANNI (b. 1943), US poet

INTRODUCTION

It may sound crazy that many change initiatives fail because the purpose of the change is insufficiently thought through. The evidence is that this may well be the case. In their engagingly funny but perceptive book on change Harvey Robbins and Michael Finley[1] produce the memorable statement:

> *'The worst reason for plunging a company into the boiling oil of change is to alleviate the boredom of senior management.'*

Unquestionably there is a syndrome affecting managers, more prevalent in the modern business environment than ever before, which produces a sense of unease, a need to intervene if things seem to be going too smoothly. In part this is caused by management fads and in part by observing competitors closely; if the competitors are doing it, shouldn't we . . .? Paranoia is, in fact, advised as we saw in Chapter 11 even by, or maybe especially by, the spokespeople of very successful organizations like Andy Grove of Intel.

It would be folly to suggest that the reasons change initiatives fail boil down to purposeless, bored, paranoid or fad-obsessed management; that would be manifestly untrue. So we must once again reassert . . .

> There is one reason, and one reason only for undertaking change in the organization and that is the better to implement its strategy. (See Chapter 2, especially Table 2.1 on change levers.)

If we start from this basic truth we are far more likely to avoid a failed change initiative because in establishing the strategy, the change will have been established as a consequence of the needs of the strategy rather than as a strategy itself.

In Chapter 7 we provided a model for planning a change programme, this chapter deals with those things which are commonly credited with (or accused of) causing a change programme to fail.

LACK OF CLARITY OF OUTCOME

Most extended change programmes involve a number of different components. For example, you may be working on process changes and structural changes at the same time. Many organizations find the change programme either becoming disjointed or running into the sand because of not having taken the time to get clarity and alignment about the destination. Successful change initiatives are characterized by having taken the time to deconstruct the change initiative into its component parts, and satisfactorily having answered the following questions.

- What does the change look like when it is working? Can we describe in detail what is different?

- What will each of these differences give us that we don't have now? How do these differences support the strategy?

- What is the consequence of our not achieving the differences we defined above? How or why will the strategy suffer as a consequence?

- How will we know that we are on track to achieve the change – are there recognizable milestones?

- How will we know that we have actually achieved the change?

- Are there honest pragmatic and authentic measures that we can apply (. . . to both the milestones and to the total change)?

Experience seems to show that the process of clarifying and describing objectives actually minimizes their number. It is not clear why this happens beyond the possibility that a team framing the kinds of objectives needed to plan implementation are often carried away on the crest of a euphoric wave. As the reality and potential difficulty of enacting change starts to become apparent, more achievable and pragmatic decisions are taken.

Experience seems to show that the process of clarifying and describing objectives actually minimizes their number.

There is also a positive correlation between success and involvement. In other words, if those who have actually to achieve a component of the change are involved in both defining its outcome (what it looks like) and how things are different as a result, then the objectives set will have two characteristics:

- they are more likely to be achieved

- they are often more ambitious than those set by a manager on a top down basis.

The broad lesson to avoid disaster seems to be that the greater the level of involvement before the change gun is fired, the higher the likelihood of success.

It is often true that a change initiative has to be embarked upon before the metrics can be devised. This is not a recipe for disaster, provided the organization is clear about what it is they will measure, even if a base level measure has not yet been established and an aspirational or planned improvement cannot yet be predicated. It is sufficient to say what the organization will measure it and why. 'How' can follow, and sometimes those closest to the change can provide the good advice and insight that delivers the 'how'. What does not work is to drop in an unplanned measure at a later date giving the impression of confronting your people with a 'gotcha'.

The implementation programme should seek to minimize the time that those affected by the change can express negativity towards it and spend their energy finding reasons to prove that it will not work rather than getting on with making it work.

FACTORS WHICH CONTRIBUTE TO AN INADEQUATE IMPLEMENTATION PROGRAMME

Allowing insufficient time

Anybody who has been involved in a large change initiative will tell you that it takes much longer than anticipated; it moves more slowly than one is likely to imagine even with this advice. If you look again at Chapter 6, which outlines the process people go through in accepting and enacting change, you get an idea of why it often takes a long time.

The implementation programme should seek to minimize the time that those affected by the change can express negativity towards it and spend their energy finding reasons to prove that it will not work rather than getting on with making it work. The advice offered in Chapter 6 will help curtail this period of instability.

Lack of co-ordination

Above all, a change initiative which is happening at a number of levels on a number of fronts needs to be supported by managerial behaviour which unambiguously supports the changes sought and demonstrates the new criteria which prevail.

Successful implementation means that a number of change enablers have to be synchronized so that they work together. There is no sense, for example, in making structural changes in the organization if the objectives (and rewards for achieving them) are not recast to reflect the purpose of the new structure. There is no point in altering the hierarchy without clear redefinition of the processes that the new hierarchy is supposed to support. Above all, a change initiative which is happening at a number of levels on a number of fronts needs to be supported by managerial behaviour which unambiguously supports the changes sought and demonstrates the new criteria which prevail.

Insufficient or inappropriate communication

If the time taken to enact change always exceeds expectation, so too is the degree of communication needed. To cascade the information about a change: what it is, why we are doing it, and how we are going about it, through an organization is not a one-time activity. Rather it is a sustained, ongoing communications programme, which must be thoroughly thought through. It must also be consistently monitored so that the organization clearly understands the effect that the communication is having.

New opportunities and new media must be found to repeat the message. New ways must be found to convey the same message with greater meaning and relevance to those who hear it. Chapter 6 provides a stage by stage programme for change leaders, and the advice it offers stems from the frequency with which we encounter change initiatives which have come to nothing because the supporting communication programme has run out of steam and people have lost interest in it.

Lack of perceived energy and tenacity

To convince a shrewd and often cynical group of employees that a change must be taken seriously, those responsible for leading it will have to demonstrate great energy and resolve in supporting it. If there is a history of change initiatives having fizzled out in the organization, it becomes even more necessary for everyone, but especially the senior people, to demonstrate consistently that they are working at it, pushing it forward, finding ways of making it work, etc. Remember it is the observed behaviour which defines the culture; if the change is to be taken seriously those responsible for it must be seen to sweat a bit.

In most of the post mortem examinations I have conducted of change initiatives that expired, a central reason is that the management failed to evince a sufficiently consistent and energetic effort in their support.

Inadequate resources

Many change initiatives are introduced in order to save money. This is particularly true of Business Process Re-engineering (BPR) which has a reputation for being introduced to shed overheads rather than, as claimed, to shed redundant processes. When cost reduction is at the heart of the change, the organization is often reluctant (and sometimes unable) to devote the resources to powering the change process along. This can mean that communication forums are curtailed, retraining is skimped, supporting IT (on which a great deal of change is predicated), is inadequate and so on.

Dealing with, and implementing new practices and processes often costs employees considerable effort and time. The organization, if it is to be credible in the eyes of its people, must provide the resources to cover that lost time. This may mean consultants, part-time help, temporary outsourcing, etc.

Failed change initiatives usually leave employees with the perception that they now have an enlarged job and responsibility, and an increased workload. The only beneficiary is the company's bottom line. This is a recipe for discontent, cynicism and often non co-operation.

Tangible resources being devoted to the change convey a message of

Tangible resources being devoted to the change convey a message of authenticity to the workforce as well as providing the ability to support those things which will enable or speed up the change process.

authenticity to the workforce as well as providing the ability to support those things which will enable or speed up the change process.

Lack of organizational readiness

Earlier in this book I have mentioned, and increasingly in day-to-day consultancy I have encountered, organizations which are punch drunk with change. Too much has happened too often for the organization to regroup itself and to consolidate and digest what has happened to it. Sometimes organizations just seem exhausted and depleted, simply lacking the energy to deal with another bout of change.

Another cause for lack of readiness is that the organization at large simply does not understand why the changes are necessary. This is usually a failure of communication and requires the change leaders to make convincing and eloquent cases for what is happening. In the end, it is only if the change and the reasons for it have high face validity in the eyes of the employees that it stands a chance of being achieved.

Rhetoric, even gifted oratory, has less effect on the employees than a clear understanding of the realities the organization is facing and the strategy that is being implemented to address the situation.

In organizations with powerful middle management strata there is often a predisposition towards the preservation of empires. You might isolate this in a force field analysis (see Chapter 7) but it might be harder to identify the subtlety and versatility of resistance which can be encountered.

WHY *KAIZEN*-BASED CHANGE INITIATIVES FAIL

It will come as no surprise to discover that installing *Kaizen* in the organization is just as prone to failure as any other kind of change programme. One can even argue that developing a *Kaizen* culture takes even longer than, for example, to restructure from a functionally-based organization to a customer-based structure. The reason it takes longer is that a *Kaizen*-based organizational culture rests on synthesizing and co-ordinating a number of components to install it. In brief these are as follows.

- Team-based thinking, performing and hence team-based organization.

- The use of a high degree of cross functionality.
- A process-based focus which sometimes takes longer to demonstrate convincingly that it is by incremental change that substantial improvement is created.
- A philosophy which, while competitive, is governed by rules of mutual support, mutual respect, honesty and constructive confrontation.
- Developing competence in the underlying *Kaizen* tools like root cause analysis, waste elimination, the 5 Ms of managing at *gemba*, the 5 Ss of good house-keeping, PDCA and SDCA, etc.

These disciplines, of themselves, take some absorbing and their application in the workplace requires experimentation, and, even granted goodwill by employees, there is a limited amount of time that trust in their potential can be sustained before tangible evidence of their success will be required.

Granted that installing *Kaizen* in an organization is long, arduous and requires possibly more commitment than more limited change initiatives, once embedded, the organization's preparedness and capacity to change is enormously enhanced.

HOW DO YOU KNOW WHEN THINGS GO WRONG?

Given that most change initiatives are launched on already hard working employees who, not being silly, quickly realize that this is going to mean more, different and changed work, the announcement of a major change is rarely received with approbation. That is not to say that the intent of the initiative will not be understood, sometimes even the necessity will be acknowledged, and possibly the change itself welcomed. Even if positively received, this is not, as I have repeatedly warned, any indication that the change will be enacted and implemented with enthusiasm and energy.

A static to negative climate almost always surrounds the early days of change and, as we have seen earlier it takes a while for the momentum to start. The judgement call is how we know, in this negative climate, whether the initiative is failing or simply has not yet reached the defining events which precede enactment.

The other judgement call required of the change leaders is whether the benefits being produced are sustainable long term and contributing positively to the implementation of organizational strategy. A few positive indicators of success will not necessarily provide immutable proof of long-term strategic effectiveness. (Though you should probably celebrate any success to reinforce its achievement and to generate more change momentum.) In short management has to know:

- that the change initiative is being implemented
- that it is delivering the anticipated result.

Here are three tell-tale signs that things are not going well:

- stressed people
- failure to meet expectations
- collateral damage.

Stressed people

Gauging the amount of stress people in the organization are feeling is a key skill for the change leader. What must be prevented is the organization moving from stretch to stress. Indicators of incipient stress are that some people become withdrawn and uncommunicative, others become voluble and combative. Pockets of disaffection and dysfunction develop and, if not dealt with the problem becomes organization-wide. Often the deterioration of morale is exacerbated if the change initiative requires a loss of jobs. Tough as it is for the leavers, the survivors also require active rehabilitation and therapy to restore their confidence, to assuage the guilt they may feel for being survivors, and to restore their confidence in their managers.

Productivity in a stressed organization plummets, absenteeism rockets and staff turnover increases. The culture becomes cynical, resistant and unco-operative. This will bring almost all change initiatives to a shuddering halt, worse, it will seriously diminish the ability of any organization to operate productively. The situation will take ages to cure and may require a substantial renewal of people to change the culture.

Few organizations reach this stage, but some come close to it, closer than normally intelligent managers should allow. It is a characteristic of an organization sliding into stress that managers become defensive of their position and remote from and insensitive to the plight of their employees. The organization polarizes into 'them and us' camps. In this condition radical intervention is needed – see later in this chapter.

Importantly the employees must be sensitively and acutely observed because it is their behaviour that is likely to provide the least ambiguous early warning sign of the change initiative running into trouble.

Failure to meet expectations

Earlier in this chapter we discussed the importance of getting alignment about how the success of the change initiative would be judged and measured both at the milestone level and at the final outcome level. Without these points of orientation to check against it becomes difficult to decide whether the initiative is on course. If these measures have not been agreed, then it is virtually impossible to hold a rational discussion with employees about what is happening and what to do about it. If agreed measures exist, and targets are not being met, the basis of a dialogue has been provided and with this comes the opportunity for remedial action. Conversely, if agreed measures are being achieved or exceeded this provides useful opportunities for celebratory feedback and reinforcement.

The important thing to follow through on in any change initiative is performance against goals, objectives or expectations.

The important thing to follow through on in any change initiative is performance against goals, objectives or expectations. Without measuring, organizations are incapable of making informed judgements about whether the change is being implemented or whether it is working to support the desired strategic outcome.

> *The disciplines of Kaizen's Plan Do Check Act (PDCA) greatly aid the process of change initiatives. The use of standards through the SDCA routine helps 'bank' the success being achieved and to consolidate it into practice.*

Collateral damage

Among the early indications of trouble might well be the emergence of problems in operating units which may not be directly dealing with the change but are affected by it. It is not unusual to discover that an eliminated work process in unit A produces a compensatory need in unit B. This happens because the complexity of entire work flows in organizations often exceeds the knowledge of even a group of people familiar with parts of it. Ordinarily these problems will be relatively easily solved.

In those situations where operating criteria are radically altered in an unforeseen or unplanned way we get collateral damage. This problem need not be insoluble but if the extent becomes widespread, we may have made some fundamental miscalculations in the change we have planned.

It is a frequent experience in Businesses Process Re-engineering that the 'elimination of non value-adding activities' results in expensive compensatory activities elsewhere within the organization. It is also often the case that change leaders do not move to solve or even acknowledge the problem and leave it to be dealt with at an operational level. This practice, more than any other, is responsible for the stress which is more widely reported in organizations – see Chapter 1.

Another manifestation of collateral damage is the fairly widespread practice of eliminating positions within the organization in favour of outsourcing. The people who have been eliminated are then re-employed as consultants, sometimes at higher cost, often at greater risk to the organization.

> *Kaizen's stress on cross-functionality and focus at the process level is particularly well suited to the anticipation of collateral damage. Further the philosophy of the next person in the process being the customer, really helps to locate the most appropriate place in the value chain to provide the 'fix'.*

WHAT TO DO WHEN THINGS GO WRONG

Take a decision!

It is often extremely difficult for the change leaders or senior people within the organization to do the mind shift from implementing the change to repairing the damage. It is, understandably, difficult to adjust to the completely different agenda that is required. In many cases the failure of the change initiative is seen as a defeat, reputations may be at stake and jobs may be on the line. Often there are substantial financial penalties involved, sometimes the organization is in a mess with back-logs of work, dissatisfied customers and, almost always, dispirited employees.

This is a classic time for a change of senior executives, and, if the change has been much touted or had much riding upon it, it is not unusual for investors or directors to demand a sacrifice. It is also often easier for a new incumbent to start the repair process than somebody who has been central to the change process in the past.

Whatever the circumstances surrounding it, it is essential that the decision is taken to stop the change process and start to repair the damage.

Assess the damage

The next step is to assess the damage. Typically there are obvious manifestations like backlog, cost overruns, customer complaints, etc. The damage assessment should also plumb attitudes within the company, it should seek to measure what has happened to the culture, and it should look at communications, at morale, at motivation and so on.

It should also look at the organization's strategy. Is the strategic intent which lay behind the change still valid or was it misjudged? Was it the implementation of the change or was it the strategy that was at fault?

Sometimes it is difficult to take the time to assemble the degree and depth of detail required. In the end it is essential that this is comprehensively done for it becomes the basis on which the damage repair programme will be designed.

Announce the transition from change to repair and restoration

It is important to signal unambiguously to the whole organization that a new era is inaugurated, that a new set of priorities have emerged, that what will now happen is that the organization will work to restore stability rather than implement change.

Do not expect that this will be greeted with relief or delight. More than likely, your people will be further antagonized by further change. Lots of recrimination gets released, lots of '. . . I told you so . . .' gets uttered.

Design the repair and restoration programme

What you now engage in is the exact image of the original change plan, i.e.:

- determine and get agreement on the outcomes you are seeking
- determine the criteria, measures and metrics that will be used
- enlist your people in the planning and implementation
- fire the gun and start.

The essence of this activity is around clear and agreed outcomes to solicit as much involvement, contribution and assistance and help as you can. The more participation you can solicit the smoother will be the repair programme. Sometimes it helps, as with the change planning process, to identify a champion or a group who become the movers and shakers. As with change implementation we celebrate successes in the journey to repair, as with the change programme we try by all means possible to maintain high communication, urgency and momentum.

KEY POINTS

The main reasons for change initiatives failing in an organization are as follows.

- Making changes for any reason other than to support the strategy.
- Failing to establish clarity of outcome.
- Implementing an inadequate change programme, specifically:
  - allowing insufficient time
  - lack of co-ordination
  - insufficient or inappropriate communication
  - managers perceived as lacking the energy and tenacity to effect the change.
- Inadequate resources being devoted to the change process.
- Lack of organizational readiness.

You can tell that things are going wrong when you see the following.

- The organization showing signs of stress.
- Objectives not being met.
- Collateral damage starting to happen.

If things are going wrong do the following.

- Decide to do a mind shift from managing change to repairing damage.
- Assess the damage.
- Make the announcement about the shift.
- Devise the same kind of plan you would devise to effect change but this time direct it at making good the damage.
- Enlist the people in the plan.

Note

1.   Robbins, H. and Finley, M. (1997) *Why Change Doesn't Work, Why Initiatives go Wrong and How to Try Again – and Succeed*, Orion Business.

INDEX